SPEAKING OF
ATLANTIC CITY

SPEAKING OF
ATLANTIC CITY

· Recollections & Memories ·

COMPILED BY JANET ROBINSON BODOFF AND LEESA TOSCANO

THE
History
PRESS

Published by The History Press
Charleston, SC
www.historypress.com

Front cover, top: David Rosen. *Bottom*: John Margolies Roadside America photograph archive (1972–2008), Library of Congress, Prints and Photographs Division. *Back cover, inset*: David Rosen. *Bottom*: Authors' collection.

First published 2022

Manufactured in the United States

ISBN 9781467150743

Library of Congress Control Number: 2022939456

Notice: The information in this book is true and complete to the best of our knowledge. It is offered without guarantee on the part of the authors or The History Press. The authors and The History Press disclaim all liability in connection with the use of this book.

This anthology is dedicated to the late Pauline Renchon, the first person interviewed for Speaking of Atlantic City: Recollections and Memories, *with appreciation for her support of this project. It is also dedicated in loving memory of Lisa Jae Melaragni, who lived in and loved Atlantic City.*

CONTENTS

CONTENTS

Contents

PREFACE

For more than 150 years, people have been coming to Atlantic City, New Jersey, to bathe in the ocean, walk on the boardwalk and get away from their day-to-day lives. Herein are the stories of some of those people and some of the people who greeted them when they arrived.

The arts community is very active in the Atlantic City area, and many of our local writers and photographers as well as those who have visited the shore have contributed to the recollections in this anthology.

We hope that some of our stories bring back your memories of days in the sun and sand on our shores.

—Janet Robinson Bodoff and Leesa Toscano

Opposite, left: Melissa Webb and Alex Monti on the beach. *Photo by Stephanie Monti.*

Opposite, right: Sherrise Moten enjoys a refreshing dip in the ocean. *Photo by Gary Moten.*

ACKNOWLEDGEMENTS

Our thanks to the many people who have made this anthology possible:

Editors
Janet Robinson Bodoff
Tery Lever

Contributing Writers
Shelley Andress-Cohen
Meryl Baer
Janet Robinson Bodoff
I.R. Cartagena
Phyllis Rita Cinquino
Emari DiGiorgio
Pat Hanahoe-Dosch
Puneett Dutt
Gail Fishman Gerwin
Molly Golubcow
Bob Ingram
Lucy Jerue

Suzanne Koiro
Bob Levin
Barry Levy
Elinor Mattern
Morgan Mulloy
Turiya S.A. Raheem
Jessy Randall
Enid Shomer
Leesa Toscano
Nicole Warchol
Richard K. Weems
Laryssa Wirstiuk

Contributing Photographers

Ines Bloom
Janet Robinson Bodoff
Molly Golubcow
Kristian Gonyea
Bernard Jenkins
Merill Kelem
Stephanie Monti

Gary Moten
David Rosen
Harriet Segal
Shaun R. Smith
Sandy Stoltzman
Leesa Toscano

Chapter 1

BORN TO THE RESTAURANT BUSINESS

Janet Robinson Bodoff

*P*auline Bromberg Renshon was born in 1937 and grew up in Atlantic City. Her father, Meyer, was a restaurateur, and she worked in his restaurants throughout her childhood and into her adulthood. Over the years, Meyer Bromberg owned a series of coffee shops in Atlantic City, and Pauline worked in every one of them.

Until fourth grade, Pauline lived above her father's luncheonette, the Four Twos, and helped out wherever she could. It was located at 2222 Pacific Avenue between Columbia Place and Missouri Avenue and from there derived its name. In a neighborhood peppered with small mom-and-pop businesses, the Brombergs were surrounded with families earning their livings by chipping in and working hard.

Next door to the Four Twos was a fruit and produce business, next to it was Tripichin's Rooming House, across the street was a hot dog and hamburger stand, a few doors down was Tutor's Barber Shop and Tripichin's candy store was nearby on the boardwalk.

Pauline's uncles, her mother's siblings, the Fishman brothers, owned gas stations all over town; Uncles Irv and Dave had a Super Service on Tennessee Avenue, Uncle Fred had a Sunoco at Michigan and Atlantic and Uncle Al had an Amoco station on Albany Avenue.

In her time off, Pauline discovered her city and her neighbors as they discovered her. On the corner of Mississippi and Atlantic was the Babette Club, a typical 1940s nightclub with showgirls and cabaret entertainment. Pauline had long, silky blonde hair, and when she would wander into

Babette's during the day and sit on top of the piano, one or another of the showgirls would plait her hair.

For a little girl growing up at the seashore, the war years left many vivid memories. Pauline recalled the sight of air raid wardens walking along the boardwalk and streets of Atlantic City. The air raid wardens made sure that everyone had their blackout shades thoroughly covering their windows so that no lights would show in the night. In case the Nazis flew over the Jersey shore, they would find no targets in Atlantic City.

The air raid wardens handed out gas masks in case of attacks that, happily, never came. But war scares never stopped tourists from seeking entertainment, eating at restaurants or visiting movie theaters. People came to the shore to stroll on the boardwalk or bathe at the beach, and when they were hungry, they ate. Pauline and her family continued to serve them.

The war left Atlantic City with no harm done, but the fall of 1944 saw the arrival of disastrous devastation. The Great Atlantic Hurricane of 1944 did enormous damage. Piers were washed away; water flooded the streets; and when the storm ended, the green newsstand in front of the Four Twos coffee shop was found four blocks away on Florida Avenue. The Bromberg brothers had to cart it back, laughing and swearing all the way.

When her dad opened Meyer's Hot Dog Stand on the boardwalk, Pauline, again, pitched in. That summer, she was ten, and she spent her days walking up and down the boardwalk covered in a sandwich board that hung over her shoulders and proclaimed "Come Get Your Red Hot, Hot Dogs at Meyer's Hot Dog Stand."

Eventually, her dad moved the coffee shop to the boardwalk at 1 South New York Avenue in the Schwehm Building, where she was a waitress after school and during the summers. Busy days and nights came and went as employment in the family business continued.

For many years in the early 1900s, the back of Young's Million Dollar Pier held the Crystal Ballroom, a mirrored palace-like gathering place that was the venue for many cotillion dances. Young men, women and children would arrive in their best attire and parade around the room before the band would play, and people would dance the afternoon away. When George Hamid purchased the pier, it became an amusement wonderland for kids as well as adults. Hamid's Million Dollar Pier held a wide variety of pleasures for kids, a beautifully ornate merry-go-round, a colorful tilt-a-whirl, smashing bumper cars and a myriad of games of chance at which you could win all types of giant stuffed animals and toys. For grown-ups, there was a burlesque show at the very back of the pier that

Pauline and her friends always tried to sneak into. It, too, was washed away in the 1944 hurricane.

The only Jewish girl in an Italian neighborhood, Pauline often encountered prejudice. The local nuns from Saint Michael's Church befriended her. They lived in a boardinghouse around the corner and afforded her some friendly support as well as some tasty snacks. After some business success, in 1944, her family moved to a big, beautiful home on LaClede Place in lower Chelsea, a well-appointed neighborhood of lovely single homes. It was a large, six-bedroom house with a two-bedroom basement apartment. They had moved, but hatred moved with them. Anti-Semitism was rampant in America in those years. One day, the family came home from work and saw that someone had painted "Jew go home" on the front of the house. They cleaned it up and carried on.

Homes in the 1930s and '40s often had a telephone party line. Sometimes when you picked up the phone to make a call, you would hear a neighbor having a conversation. Sometimes you listened in. On the other end of the Bromberg party line was an area bookie. Often Pauline would pick up the phone to make a call and hear horses racing and the sound of a man calling the race.

Many families who lived in Atlantic City year-round earned some extra money by renting out their homes to vacationers in the summer. Pauline's family was no different. For several years after moving to LaClede Place, they would move to an apartment above the Bella Napoli Restaurant so they could rent their home to summer visitors. Finally, when she was eleven, her parents decided to move into their own two-bedroom basement apartment. Unfortunately, unknown to them, their neighborhood had been converted to a triple-A zone, which meant that their single-family home had been converted from a two-family home, and only one family could legally occupy it. They found out the legalities of their living situation when they were evicted at three o'clock one morning and taken to jail. Happily, Pauline's dad had a friend in California, and they spent the rest of the summer in Burbank. Unfortunately, the friend's accommodations included black widow spiders that loved the dark. Pauline went to bed every night for the rest of the summer with a flashlight. Needless to say, she was very happy to return home to Atlantic City.

By the time Pauline was in her twenties, she had worked various jobs at many of her dad's businesses. When her father, Meyer, opened Woofie's in 1955 on the ground floor of the Teplitsky's Hotel, she continued her career as a waitress. One afternoon, the colorful red-and-turquoise booths were full to capacity. While the place was packed with hungry vacationers, it was stormed by black-suited, gun-flailing FBI agents who were looking for Fred Teplitsky. The patrons and employees alike were unnerved, but, thankfully, the problems were not theirs—although the Brombergs and their businesses were not trouble-free.

Meyer Bloomberg kept money for taxes in the walk-in freezer. Talk about cold cash…and his employees did. One day one, of the restaurant's cooks, named Cherry, pulled a gun on Meyer, trying to rob the place, but Meyer was able to overcome the situation, and Cherry went to jail.

And when the union tried to organize Woofie's, there was more trouble. When Pauline's mother tried to get into the restaurant to work, she ended up at Atlantic City Hospital with a broken jaw. Pauline's younger brother, Fred, heard this and went to Woofie's with a spiked ball-and-chain, but he was too late to save a nun from injury. The nun put her hand on the door to get in to get something to eat and left without a meal but with a broken wrist.

Meyer joined with other restaurant owners, including Mr. Latz from Latz's Knife and Fork Inn, and hired a lawyer. They were unable to affect the situation to their benefit, and the whole mess eventually fizzled out.

Pauline's dad passed away in 1955, and as a result, so did the restaurants and Pauline's career as a waitress.

Chapter 2

ARRIVALS

Turiya S.A. Raheem

AUTHOR'S NOTE: My grandparents, Alma and Clifton Washington, started Wash's Restaurant in 1937 as a tiny sandwich shop not far from Atlantic City's famous Club Harlem. Eventually, business outgrew the sandwich shop, and they moved to 1702 Arctic Avenue and had a full-service seafood restaurant for about twenty-five years before the city's decline caused my uncle to move the place to Pleasantville, New Jersey.

My grandparents first arrived in Atlantic City full of hope for a better future than what they might have had in Dinwiddie County, Virginia, a Jim Crow area in 1920s America. Neither had a restaurant background, but they both had some college, were willing to work hard and loved the thought of a family business. They achieved their dream, and the family business lasted seventy-five years, employing four generations of Washingtons and an untold number of local residents as well.

This is the story of their arrival in their new home.

*M*arie and I hugged each other desperately after being away from each other for more than two years. Her sight had been off and on since she was fifteen or so, but she squinted over my shoulder as we hugged, and I could feel her listening to the neighborhood, surveying the place we would call home and where we would raise our eleven children—my seven and her four. As I watched her at the window, I recalled the first time I saw what seemed to be one continuous row of pastel, wood-

Above: Wash's Sandwich Shop lunch counter. *Courtesy of Washington family.*

Opposite: Alma and Clifton Washington celebrate their twenty-fifth wedding anniversary with friends and family. *Courtesy of Washington family.*

frame houses for as far as my eyes could see, with few open spaces like back in McKenney. I knew she was remembering how back home in Virginia, we had to walk at least half a mile to visit our next-door neighbors, most of whom were kinfolk of one sort or another. Atlantic City was noisy with people living so close up to one another. Marie was listening to the noises of the neighborhood.

"Me and Charlie hardly spoke on the train ride up," she finally said.

"I guess y'all were too excited," I smiled, standing close to my big sister as I placed slices of pound cake on small plates. "Come on, sit here."

"Yes, excited and nervous at the same time. The air on that train was so thick with humidity. Charlie described the dusty roads, fields and fields of tobacco and all sorts of vegetables as we passed through Virginia, Maryland and Delaware."

"I know you could picture the beauty of it all. Turned to lush green scenery as you got further and further north, didn't it?" I asked, remembering the train ride Clif and I had taken.

"Yes, indeed. We lost count of all the farms and towns spread out behind the tiny rail stations. Next thing you know, we're pulling into the station in Philadelphia," she smiled. "I bet this kitchen looks just like Momma's," she laughed.

"You know me too well, Marie," I laughed. "I sewed some of those same red-and-white-checkered curtains and hung them up to these two small windows. Found a matching tablecloth, too, and some red vinyl chairs."

"I can tell. You must have a nice landlady."

"Oh, she was glad when I fixed the place up like this. Reminded her of her own home back in Richmond," I told Marie, as we sat down at the table in the middle of the kitchen. "Let me take this to Charlie and Clif. I'll be right back."

"Mertina is more beautiful than I even remember, Marie," I announced, returning to the kitchen. "Out there up under her daddy, looking like a miniature Lena Horne."

"Yes, she is a daddy's girl," Marie laughed. She was at one of the windows again, watching and listening to children playing in the alley.

"You have an icebox in this window, don't you?"

"Yes, indeed, small but nice to have one," I answered.

"Lots of children around here, too," she continued, while making her way back to the table.

"Good children though. I think they get responsible early 'cause their parents are always working," I told her. "I'm so glad y'all are here now."

"Me too," she said and reached across the table to caress my hand. "Every time somebody back home got another letter about how much money could be made in Atlantic City, I was hoping it would be our turn next."

"I know. You don't know whether to believe people or not, but we found work pretty fast thanks to Ruby Lee and Robert. Atlantic City has enough jobs for everybody willing to work, and lots of colored tourists come with money to spend on family vacations."

"Ain't that somethin'," Marie remarked. "Charlie said when we pulled into the station in Philadelphia, coloreds and whites mixed all together."

"I remember. The north has become the place to be after Reconstruction and all that Jim Crow foolishness. Nobody's putting up with that stuff if they don't have to. There are lots more opportunities for good housing, better jobs and higher education up here."

"So can we teach school since we have some college education?"

"I haven't looked into it yet. I got some more news for you," I laughed, quietly this time.

"I know that laugh," said Marie. "Pregnant, ain't you?"

"Yes, pregnant again."

We ate the cake I had baked in honor of their arrival and talked about how glad we were that our parents had seen to it that their daughters got schooling at Dinwiddie Vocational and Virginia Normal and Collegiate Institute. They must have known that all them white men in Virginia wanted to reconstruct was slavery under the new name of *sharecropping*. We missed Momma and Daddy and our four brothers, but mostly we missed our sisters: Lillie, Courtney, Hazel, Sadie and Alese. What we didn't miss was that red-haired, green-eyed white man who visited now and again with bags of food and used clothing. We had suspected that he was our grandpa, but no one ever confirmed it for us. He'd drop by the farm from time to time when Poppa wasn't at home, give Momma the things he'd brought, walk around a bit and then leave without ever saying one word.

As Marie updated me on everyone, I was glad Clif had wanted to come to New Jersey. Colored folks in Baltimore acted too uppity for me, and New York sounded too big and crowded for anyone from Dinwiddie County. While riding the train, I had thought about how we could have made a life for ourselves in McKenney or even Petersburg, maybe. I could've kept teaching the children from the surrounding farms, and maybe Clif would've become a dentist eventually. We would have been well respected and built ourselves a fine home for our family. Of course, I didn't tell him any of this as the train rattled its way on up the East Coast. He had gotten tired of farming life and southern white folks some time ago and set his sights on the North Star. With some college education and society becoming more and more industrialized, he dreamed of all kinds of possibilities. White men might have been a pain in the neck, but they were not an obstacle to my husband. When his big sister, Ruby Lee, wrote to him extolling the many opportunities to be found in Atlantic City, New Jersey, he knew we had to at least give the place a try. I figured Atlantic City was enough city for me, and now that Marie was here, I was sure everything would be just fine.

Marie yanked the thick braids crossed on top of my head with a familiar fondness, and we laughed, listening to the people shouting out of windows to the man with vegetables on the back of his truck, the fish man yelling his sale for the day and the mothers yelling for their children to come in and eat. Later, we walked over to Ruby Lee's. She and Bobby had been living in AC for almost ten years, and Bobby had worked his way up at Kent's Restaurant. Before they bought their own house, we all lived at the same boardinghouse; three of five young couples were from Virginia, so it felt kind of like home. Each couple had their own bedroom, but we had to share a small parlor and the kitchen and bathroom facilities. Still, we were happy to be done with outhouses. I remember thinking when I used that old outhouse that the greenhead flies on this island would have chewed my bottom to pieces, and around every corner there were salty marshes I knew must be full of mosquitoes or some other disease-carrying creatures. The scent of saltwater owned the air in this beach town that felt like an urban center.

The first time I put my toes in that soft, beige sand, burning the soles of my feet in the midday sun, I felt maybe I could make AC my home. As we boarded the Camden-Atlantic that chugged farther and farther east toward the Atlantic Ocean, rivers and swamps led into ever-larger bodies of water in the distance, until the greatest expanse of water I had ever seen gleamed in the sunlight, so far out that I thought I could see all the way to Africa. I wondered about those waves in a frightened way, even though I knew how to swim, and wondered if I'd be able to plant me a garden in the sandy soil here.

Clif and I had strolled over from the Northside, then across Atlantic Avenue, which was so wide it had cars on both sides of the street and train tracks down its middle. We crossed the wood planks people called the *boardwalk* and went on down to the edge of the shore and removed our shoes and socks. We strolled along the colored section of the beach at Missouri Avenue and listened to the timeless rhythm of rolling waves swishing coolly over our feet. They crashed and receded, crashed and receded, with a monotonous melody that you knew had been around even before the creation of Adam and Eve. The water in our bodies seemed to take on the same rhythm as we walked in silence, Clifton empty of his usual easy conversation, our hearts smiling at our new beginnings. I think we knew we were a tad bit afraid. We were oblivious to the colored sunbathers congregating on blankets and towels and in the surf all around us. As the sun crept higher into the sky, we hurried back over the hot sand to where we'd started, retrieved our socks and shoes and headed back toward the boardinghouse, the first of many places we would live for a couple of years.

When we reached the promenade everyone called the boardwalk, we were astonished to find throngs of people, young and old, colored and white, families and singles and couples, all immersed in various types of entertainment. We hadn't noticed before that people were dressed in their finest clothes, what we called *Sunday best*, having changed out of their bathing suits and stockings at one of the many nearby bathhouses. Women carried ruffled parasols, and children ate cotton candy, while men smoked hefty, brown cigars. Families seemed to be celebrating some sort of holiday. There were twinkling red, green, blue and yellow lights everywhere, and game bells rang out for winners, clowns juggled balls high into the air, musicians played horns and drums and fancy ladies danced gaily near the bands. I could hardly believe my eyes. I recall Clifton looking at me as if to say, "See what I told you," but he knew he was as overwhelmed as I was. Atlantic City was the place to be, better than Philadelphia or New York City, even. It held the promise of long-term work as waiters, waitresses, cooks, porters, doormen, bellhops, busboys, chambermaids and more, and there was room for advancement in every field, especially if you were educated. Ruby Lee and Bobby said plenty of colored people were already buying houses, cars and modern appliances and owning their own businesses, too, all on the Northside. As we walked home, it was clear to us that this city could not survive or progress without our community, and Clif and I aimed to get a piece of this American dream, too.

With all the excitement of our new hometown, we hardly had time to notice that America was headed toward the Great Depression. We started out working odd jobs until I became a busy housewife with a house full of children that needed disciplining, teaching, cleaning and feeding. Clif took every kind of job he could find to keep our mouths fed, our family sheltered. There were all types of benevolent associations on the Northside, dedicated to helping colored folks get settled—the Good Samaritans, the Elks, the Masons, Ladies of the Eastern Star—but we had family.

It was estimated that close to one million Negroes had left the south around the same time as we did; most were enticed to Detroit, Chicago and Pittsburgh, but on the East Coast, everyone mostly followed the railroads straight up to Baltimore, Philadelphia and New York. Philly became the second-largest urban center in the country, and when factories started closing up there because of the stock market crash, even more people headed to AC to find work, if only seasonal. Competition for jobs became harder and harder, and our children became hungrier and hungrier.

Chapter 3

CAUGHT IN THE STORM

Suzanne Koiro

Residents of the small community of Longport awoke on September, 14, 1944, to one of the worst hurricanes on record. Warnings were disregarded, as previous forecasts of impending storms had proven to be false alarms.

*L*ily telephoned Laura Mae shortly before the electricity went out and tried to hide the nervousness she felt.

"Hey, girl. Looks like we are in for a hurricane."

"Oh, right! That's what they said last week and two weeks before, remember?"

Lily was from Jamaica, where she had been through several hurricanes. She knew they weren't anything to mess with.

Laura Mae was from Georgia. She had never been in a hurricane. She thought if the weather got too bad, she and Lily could just take the trolley back to Atlantic City, like they had been doing every week for the past five years.

Lily and Laura Mae were domestics for families who each had homes in Longport. The women had struck up a friendship during the half-hour rides to and from work.

Although there had been a steady rain since they arrived at their respective homes, the sky was looking more and more ominous.

"Mrs. Woodland said she hasn't seen the ocean come over the bulkhead in the eight years she has lived here," Lily said, trying to reassure herself as well as Laura Mae.

Damage to the island from the Hurricane of September 14, 1944. *Private collection.*

Lily was a big woman. Her weight had inched over 250 pounds, in spite of the fact that she was a hard worker. She felt fortunate to work for such nice people and kept the house spotless.

The Woodlands' home was located on a corner lot. They were less than a block from the beach, and across the street, to the west, was the bay, under normal conditions a desirable location. Not so long ago, the area had been just sandy hills. Now, several homes dotted this peninsula.

"You give me a call if you decide we should head home, OK?"

"Sounds good to me, Laura Mae."

As the wind-whipped sand began to swirl, it beat against the beachfront homes, coating them as if the sand was shot out of a power-driven machine. Ross Winston glanced anxiously down the street toward the beach. From his vantage point, he could see the spray from encroaching waves crash against the bulkhead, soaring into the air.

Ross was an immigrant from Eastern Europe who moved to the United States with his wife and son many years ago. He struggled with learning a new language but soon found others in the same situation. They would meet at the local market and reminisce about the old country. Eventually, they adapted to the new cultures and their new homes. Ross enjoyed his job as a trolley conductor. He greeted his passengers with a warm smile and a "Good morning" or a "Good afternoon!" He had gotten to know the regulars, who often brought him a piece of fruit or a sweet roll. Ross drove the twenty-mile circuit, from Atlantic City, four times a day. He usually would hum familiar tunes from the old country, but today, September 14, 1944, was different.

Ross had an uneasy feeling as #409 headed for Longport. His dispatcher had said to just do one more run, in case any passengers wanted to return home before the storm. The wind made an eerie sound as it pressed against the windows of the trolley.

"I want to go home, too," Ross half mumbled, half prayed.

The trolley had to go to Eighteenth Street in Longport, make the loop, then head back to Atlantic City…and home.

As the trolley hastened to outrun the storm, the porcelain hand straps swayed in unison. The rain seemed to come from every direction, making visibility difficult. Ross fought the panic building in his body as he saw foam-filled waves dart across the street and tracks ahead. The bay was lapping at the road's edge, and he knew it was only a matter of minutes before the bay and the ocean would be joined as one—covering the land. With all the courage he could summon, Ross navigated the loop and headed home. The ocean had other ideas. Suddenly, the trolley came to a stop. Ross instinctively sounded the foot gong, usually used as a warning to cars or pedestrians. The clanging resonated through the trolley.

"What was that?" Lily asked.

"Sounded like a bell," Mrs. Woodland answered.

Lily looked out the window, and at first, all she saw was the rising tide and trees bowing to nature's wrath. Just as she was about to walk away, Lily caught sight of the trolley, stranded in several inches of churning water.

"That's Mr. Winston's trolley! It looks like he's stuck. We have to help him."

Lily could hardly hold onto the screen door as she made her way out of the house and into the tumultuous water. Debris was flying. Every step took enormous effort as she battled the surf. Without thinking of her own safety, Lily continued to struggle to reach Mr. Winston. Ross realized the situation was desperate. There was no way he could make it home. All he could do was hang on and hope someone heard his alarm.

"Mr. Winston! Mr. Winston!" Lily screamed.

Ross thought he was hearing things.

Trolley headed to Longport. *Private collection.*

"Lily?"

There was no time for explanations. Lily grabbed Ross's hand and headed for the Woodlands' home.

After the electricity and phone lines were restored, Lily was able to call her friend. "Hey, Laura Mae. That was some blow, wasn't it? Wait till you hear what happened."

Chapter 4

THE MERMAID BY THE INLET

I.R. Cartagena

S hh," the old man whispered to himself, trying to hold back a sly laugh. His heart raced as he crept down the hallway. He was Don José Dolores Cartagena, and he was forced to sneak around like a child. The reality of what he considered an unnecessary confinement usually angered him to the point where his blood boiled and he feared the onset of a heart attack, but not on this night. This night, his heart pounded with the joy of anticipation. He felt magic in the air and feared it was the last opportunity to share it with his granddaughter.

He nudged the sleepy little girl with a little more force than intended. His hands were stiff with age and had lost the gentle touch of his youth. She stirred for a moment and then slipped back under the thick, square patterns of her quilt. Evelyn nestled in the warmth of her bed and quickly drifted back into the comfort of her dreams. Like most nine-year-olds, she was exhausted from a long day of running around and playing childish games. Her little face was buried under a Rainbow Brite pillow and tangles of dark, curly hair sprawled out around her head.

Don Dolores refused to give up. He knew this was going to be a special night and wanted to share it with her. He would not let the opportunity slip away. Besides, she had made him promise to show her his special place, and he wasn't going to let her down.

Evelyn popped up in surprise after a few quick shakes of her shoulder. It took her a moment to focus, but a devilish grin instantly formed when she realized it was her *abuelo*, or *buelo* as she lovingly called him in Spanish. She could already tell what he was up to by the glimmer in his eye that shone in the dim light and the wide smile that brightened his appearance. Evelyn overflowed with youthful enthusiasm. She tried to jump out of bed and almost toppled over. He caught her by the arm, pulling the quilt away so her feet were free. Evelyn regained her balance and stepped down from the bed with her grandfather's assistance. She covered her mouth with her left hand to hold back the giggles and wrapped her free arm around his thin frame in a loving embrace.

They froze in place when a slight bang came from down the hall. Evelyn was terrified her mother would catch them. She was already on punishment for misbehaving—a result of gum that was accidentally dropped in her little sister's hair. She felt her punishment was already unfair and couldn't bear the thought of missing her favorite cartoons for another week.

Evelyn knew better than to sneak around at night, especially with her grandfather. She had seen him get scolded several times for wandering off without telling anyone. Her parents didn't mind the two of them spending time together, but they often told her that *buelo* was past his prime and couldn't properly watch a girl her age. She thought they were being silly. From her youthful perspective, he was the only fun grown-up in the house, and she loved their time together.

Don Dolores covered his mouth and tried to hold perfectly still. His eyes widened as an involuntary dry hack forced itself out. He dreaded the thought of breaking his promise. Even worse would be having to explain things to his daughter-in-law. He avoided her lectures at all costs, and a nightly excursion would definitely be grounds for a stern talking-to. It was bad enough she kept a watchful eye on him, constantly taking away his alcohol. She tried to stop him from drinking, but he had a hidden stash she would never find.

In that moment, Don Dolores wasn't worried about his liquor, and Evelyn didn't care about her cartoons. They feared they would miss out on a golden opportunity and didn't want it ruined before they even had a chance to start. They listened intently, but no one stirred. The seconds dragged on like hours, and they stared at each other with anxious faces obscured by shades of darkness. A few minutes passed, and all remained peaceful and quiet. The two exhaled in unison and hurriedly prepared to escape. Don Dolores zipped up Evelyn's puffy coat and strapped on her sneakers. They stepped lightly down the hall, avoiding all of the squeaky spots. Don Dolores cracked the back door open with a smooth, careful motion, and they slipped out into the bitter December night.

Evelyn marveled at her *buelo* as they paused under a streetlight. She thought he was very handsome for an old man who tended to cough a lot. He wore an all-white guayabera shirt that hung loosely over black slacks. His white fedora was perfectly fitted and tilted slightly to the right. Black-and-white dress shoes finished off the outfit, and his cologne filled the air with a wonderful scent that smelled like a sweet kind of soap.

Don Dolores looked at Evelyn with the intense green eyes that were easily his best feature. He actually only had one light green eye, but the difference wasn't very dramatic. His left eye was a dull blue and blind, but it remained almost as beautiful as the other. He shivered slightly and brushed his hands up and down his arms for warmth. He pulled out a half pint of Bacardi 151 from his pocket and took a long swig before returning his gaze to his granddaughter.

"*¿Qué pasó?*" he asked in Spanish, trying to figure out why she was staring at him. The young girl instantly translated his words into English in her head. She understood most of what he said but had some difficulty with his rural slang. Since she was born and raised in Atlantic City, English was her primary language, and she got by perfectly fine with her Spanglish. Their communication system worked well, considering their age and language differences. He spoke to her in Spanish, and she replied in English.

"Don't you need a coat?" she asked.

"Nah, Chilindrina, I like to feel the air on my skin," he said, as little clouds formed from his breath hitting the cold.

"Hey, don't call me that," she squealed. She hated being compared to the bratty character who cried all the time on the Spanish television show.

"I only mean it with love, my Chilindrina," he said. "Besides, I have my special juice to keep me warm, and *tu mamá* can't take it away from me. So please don't worry."

Don Dolores stared into her bright brown eyes, not wanting to disappoint his precious little girl. The truth was that his coat was locked away in her parents' room. They secured it there to prevent him from wandering off, but he wouldn't let that or the cold stop him.

"Are you going dancing?" she asked.

"No, no more dancing for me. I just like to look my best, especially when I'm with my favorite lady."

Evelyn blushed and looked around. She was sure he said the same thing to her grandmother, but she was happy to hear it anyway. She was his special girl, at least for the night. She had *buelo* all to herself and didn't have to share him with her little brother and sister.

They crossed the street and walked up the ramp to the boardwalk. "You can't catch me," she yelled. The two of them chased each other around for some time. Their hearts raced, and they laughed and played on the old wooden boards like children at a playground. Don Dolores did his best to keep up. Evelyn, like most children, wanted to get caught and tickled. They were immune to the cold, enveloped in their own little world, where they played all night without any worries.

Evelyn came to an abrupt halt before they got too close to the bad section. Her parents didn't let them get anywhere near it, and she wasn't willing to be more daring than she had to. They told her that part of the boardwalk had been battered by storms and never repaired. The frame, along with everything else, was mangled and bent in several different directions. Sections of boards were missing, and broken slabs of concrete could be seen underneath, along with the sand and shells from the beach. Broken yellow caution tape flapped in the wind at each end. Evelyn thought the whole thing looked like it was just waiting for the right fool to come along and try to walk across so it could collapse.

She always wanted to get to the other side and check out what was left of the crumbling building with the faded lobster on the side. There was a word next to it that started with an *H* that she couldn't make out, and that's why she simply called it the lobster place. The building let her know she was too close, and for a moment she stood next to her grandfather, and they observed the wrecked boardwalk, what was left of the building beyond and the rows of rundown apartment houses across the street.

Don Dolores placed an unsteady hand on her shoulder that sunk into the puff of her coat. "It wasn't always like this," he said in a somber tone. "People from all over the world used to come here. We had so much to offer."

"Really?" Evelyn asked in amazement.

She shivered, so her grandfather held her close as he pointed to the lobster building. His eyes were glazed over, and it seemed like he was somewhere else.

"You see what's left of the sign and the lobster there?" he asked. She simply nodded her head in agreement, anticipating the long-awaited answers to her many questions. "That used to be a restaurant called Hackney's. It was the biggest seafood restaurant in the world. They specialized in lobster and brought in shiploads fresh from the sea. The place was always packed. People waited in line down the block. It was larger than life. They had to force the tourists out before closing, and the next day a new line would be waiting for the place to open. The tourists couldn't get enough of it."

An early view of Hackney's Restaurant in the Inlet. *Private collection.*

He spun Evelyn around with a bit of excitement and maintained a look as if he could see something amazing far off in the distance. They faced the main part of the city, where the lights from some of the hotels and casinos were the only things that stood out in the darkness. The night began to grow lighter in anticipation of sunrise. The extra light made it easier to see farther away, but there wasn't much to look at. Evelyn took in the view of the rest of the inlet section. It was the only home she had ever known. The blocks were filled with broken-down houses turned into apartments. Many of them had caught fire over the years, but the remains of the structures were still there. The black, burned-out buildings were not that different from the dark brown houses that people probably shouldn't have been allowed to live in.

Don Dolores took another sip from his bottle and let out a happy grin as he came down to her level. He put his hand out like a photographer who couldn't figure out how to capture the right image and surveyed the area. "This was beachfront property," he said with a thrill in his voice. "This spot was jumping for years, and you couldn't imagine all the parties and celebrations we had back then. Everyone was in on the party, no matter what the occasion was. We were like one big family."

He paused for a moment, trying to gather his thoughts and compose himself. Men like him didn't show much emotion. He covered a few coughs, took a deep breath and continued his story. "The lighthouse used to shine bright at night, and you could see the lights from the piers all the way down here. We had one-of-a-kind attractions on the boardwalk and all sorts of entertainment. People brought their families and stayed for the summer to play in the sand and water every day and enjoy everything else we had to offer. We were 'America's Playground.'

"Most of us were attracted to the same things, except we came to find work. Life in Puerto Rico was rough, and jobs were hard to come by. We were lucky enough to be born U.S. citizens and could come and go as we pleased. Too many people headed to New York. I didn't like trying to compete with all them and being stuck in a crowded place. No way. That just wasn't for me. One day, a friend of mine told me he heard there was work out in Atlantic City and showed me some postcards. After that, I was sold. We spent what we had on plane tickets and never looked back."

"So, is that how you met grandma?" Evelyn interrupted with a shy smile.

"*Sí, niña*, she came here when she was very young, and we met at a party right over there. I had a girlfriend, but we weren't really serious, or at least I wasn't. But she didn't get along with your grandma and used to brag that, 'No *chica* can take my man.' One look at Gladys, and it was a wrap for me. I can't even remember the other girl's name."

He let out a laugh at the memory, but Evelyn found the thought of her *buelo* with any woman other than *abuela* to be yucky. The little girl shook off the thought and focused on his big, bright eyes and wide smile. The half-moon hung bright in the sky, and the stars painted the background as he reminisced and continued his tale. She loved the way his face lit up when he talked about her grandma and the rest of their family. The way he described everything seemed to Evelyn like a fairy tale come to life, but she couldn't figure out why he thought this place was so great.

"So…um, what happened?" she asked. "Why does it look like this now?"

Don Dolores looked at her little face, trying to hide his disappointment. The smile slowly faded, and sad eyes replaced the bright enthusiasm that had been there. He hung his head back slightly, draining what was left of the Bacardi. He savored every drop until the bottle was empty, then launched it at the nearest trash can. It missed and smashed into the gray metal railing. Evelyn jumped at the loud crashing sound and turned to see large shards of glass fly through the air and scatter all around the metal waste bin.

"What happened," he repeated with an angry tone. "People stopped coming is what happened. They wanted fancy vacations to Hawaii and Tahiti and whatever else became popular. It was like we wasn't good enough anymore, and when the tourists stopped coming, the jobs went away. We been struggling ever since to get by. And not just us; everybody here went through hard times. We didn't leave because this was our home. This was our new Puerto Rico in New Jersey. The inlet was our own little place in this world, and we couldn't abandon it. There's still something special here—I know it. And I don't mean those new casinos they keep building."

He instantly regained his former enthusiasm and led Evelyn over to the railing by the ocean. Carefully, he ducked between the rails and lowered

The Inlet at dawn. *Private collection.*

himself down onto the jetty. The jetty was like a pier made of individual boulders stacked next to each other. Most people only used them for fishing. The large rocks were slippery from the cold and water spray, so he secured his footing before he lowered Evelyn down. She didn't like the gritty feeling of the wet sand under her sneakers or the stinky smell of seaweed and remains of fish bait in the air, but she followed after her grandfather without hesitation.

They managed their way around the puddles and avoided the slick, algae-covered rocks. They walked until they were almost all the way to the end. The waves hit hard, and the large ones sprayed salty water everywhere. Evelyn could almost taste the briny liquid and made a sour face.

"You see out there," he yelled. Evelyn couldn't tell where he pointed, but she nodded enthusiastically anyway. "I was out here one night and there it…I mean, she was right over there. I didn't believe it at first, and don't think I'm crazy, but I saw it right there. It was a mermaid."

He scanned her face to judge the reaction. His movements were quicker, almost frantic, and there seemed to be a desperation in his plea. "I'm not crazy," he repeated. "I thought it was some drunk girl out there fooling around. I didn't have much to drink, or at least I don't think I did. Anyway, I saw something out there, and it was as real as you and me. It had these bright blue eyes. I never saw anything like them before. You could even see them in the dark. I couldn't stop staring at them. It was like I was in a trance—I was lucky she or it didn't want me to jump in, 'cause I think I would've. It was too dark to get a good look, but whatever it was gave me a wink then dove under, and that's when I saw her tail.

"I couldn't shake the feeling it gave off. It was like it had come here to enjoy the good vibe, and I had caught it by accident as it tried to get a closer look. I've held on to that feeling all my life, and I've been coming out here ever since, trying to see if it came back. It never did, and I'm afraid it's too late. There isn't anything left here except the hopes of your tired, old *abuelo*."

Don Dolores bent down to her level again, "You believe me, right?" he asked. Evelyn was completely taken by the story and grinned from ear to ear.

"Of course I do," she said. She was almost jumping from excitement and kept looking out into the water. "Can I see her?"

"I'm not sure. I only saw it that one time, but you never know." They both turned at the sound of a splash in the water. Evelyn squinted as she stared into the distance. She swore something in the water was moving around but couldn't tell what it was.

"Is that her, *buelo*?" she asked. Evelyn squealed with exhilaration, and they continued to scan the water.

"Don't get too excited, *niña*. Whatever it was is gone," he said.

Nothing in the world could've convinced Evelyn it was anything other than the mermaid. They searched the waters, and time seemed to stand still. Every movement in the distance was proof to the little girl that something was out there. The waves rolled roughly, and the wind blasted them from time to time. The stars and moon hung bright to aid them, and the temperature seemed to rise a bit in the first light of the early morning sun. Evelyn couldn't find where the mermaid went, but the scene in front of them was breathtaking.

She glanced over at her grandfather. He stood there mesmerized, and they shared the same look of awe. They were locked in the moment, as if it was made for the two of them. They searched for something magical out there, and even without the mermaid, the view was something special. They watched the sun come up over the horizon and reflect off the water like millions of tiny crystals were placed on top. Evelyn wrapped her arms around his waist and held him close.

She noticed his body trembled and he felt cold. Then everything happened too fast. Her grandfather began to cough and didn't stop. It was like he couldn't catch his breath. He leaned on Evelyn and then kneeled down so he wouldn't fall. Evelyn's face was full of fear. Don Dolores didn't want her to see him in that condition, and he returned her look with a grave expression of his own.

Evelyn screamed for help, hoping someone passing by on the boardwalk heard her. There wasn't anyone in sight. An eerie feeling forced her to look over the left side of the jetty. It was too dark to make out any details, but she swore she saw blue eyes staring at her from a distance. The eyes glowed with an unnatural energy, and a strange force beckoned her toward them. The forlorn figure watched them for a moment and then suddenly disappeared into the depths from which it came.

Voices shouted from close by, and she yelled back frantically. Evelyn recognized them and knew her parents must have heard her desperate shrieks. They were out looking for them and knew where *buelo*'s favorite spot was. Her father's strong arms swept her away. She took a final look around, and the waves were calm and still in the early morning sun. The seagulls flew by with an unusual silence, and there was no sign of anything out of the ordinary other than a strange quiet that hung in the air. She couldn't see her grandfather but was confident her uncles would get him to safety.

EVELYN WOKE UP IN the warmth of her bed and her mother's embrace. Her memory was fuzzy, and she felt exhausted.

"Where's *buelo*?" she asked.

"He's in the hospital," her mother said. "He should be alright, but you two almost scared us to death. I don't know what he was thinking, going out there like that. He was freezing. And at his age, he's lucky it wasn't worse."

Evelyn ignored the lecture that followed. She was simply happy her *buelo* was in a safe place. She considered telling her mother about the mermaid but quickly dismissed the idea. Evelyn knew nobody would believe her—not even her own family. She wondered if the mermaid had sensed their desperation or if she had come to say goodbye to an old friend. Whatever the reason was for her arrival, it would be their secret to keep. She laid her head on her mother's lap and snuggled tight against her warmth. They said a prayer for the crazy old man—that was her mother's loving term for her *buelo*.

Don José Dolores Cartagena never made it back from the hospital. He was really sick, and everyone had avoided telling Evelyn. No one could understand why he snuck out in the middle of the night in his condition. Most of her family laughed it up as his final adventure. They didn't mean any harm by it, and the laughter helped them cope with the loss. Evelyn laughed along with them, enjoying the stories they told about her grandfather

SPEAKING OF ATLANTIC CITY

and all the wild things he did. That was how they remembered him, but Evelyn knew his secret, and she would remember him on a deeper level than everyone else.

They wouldn't understand the nostalgic version of her grandfather that only she was able to witness. They would never know he wandered out at night because he only saw the beauty of the past out there and longed for those days to return. He didn't see the dark green water with too many jellyfish or the battered boardwalk and disintegrating neighborhoods. He saw the place of his youth that was vibrant and full of life. He saw a land of opportunity and hope for his family and a new home they made for themselves far away from where they came from. And he saw a beautiful mermaid by the inlet where they had shared the magic of this place together.

Chapter 5

SNOW ON THE BEACH

Janet Robinson Bodoff

The first time I saw snow on the beach, it was magical. The snow sparkled in the sunlight dancing on top of the sand like diamonds strewn out in front of me. It was on a rare February family trip to the shore. I had never before seen snow anywhere but on the Philadelphia city streets where I lived.

It had snowed the day before we left for the shore to visit my mom's aunt. My mom and dad loaded my brother and me into the family car, and off we went. It was very cold out, and there was still snow on the streets where I lived. We were bundled up in the back seat, dreaming about the fun we were going to have. Going to the shore always meant fun in the sun, playing in the sand and surf, a stroll on the boardwalk and playing arcade games.

At the corner of Arkansas and Pacific Avenues in Atlantic City where a themed casino now stands was a five-story Victorian hotel owned by my mother's aunt. We called her Tanty Anna. We always went to visit her in the summer, and a winter visit was very unusual, but there we were. There must have been some grown-up reason for the sojourn in the dead of winter, but my brother and I never gave it a thought.

When you're seven years old, lots of things seem magical, probably because there are so many firsts at that age. Arriving at the Ariel Hotel was certainly not one of them. Whenever we arrived there, we always ran up the steps and into the lobby to accept the love and affection of seldom-seen adults.

Snow blankets the beach. *Photo: Janet Robinson Bodoff.*

On that day, as soon as my dad parked the car after we arrived, we had started to beg to go to the boardwalk, thinking that the usual hustle and bustle of summer commerce would be there to welcome us.

After our hellos, they gave in to our pleas. Mom sat down to talk with her family while Dad walked us up the street. The cold air bit at our cheeks, but we didn't notice. The anticipation was too great. The hotel was less than one block from the beach and boardwalk where all sorts of treasures could be found. There was store after store selling beach toys and suntan lotion, restaurants serving every different cuisine we had ever heard of and penny arcades where tons of fun could be had for only a cent.

We went there every summer, and in the heat of August, the thought of snow didn't exist. That beach was a place I ran over, flying as fast as I could to get across to the edge of the ocean so as not to burn my feet.

But the boardwalk was empty. The stores were shuttered down for the winter. No other soul was there. I ran to the railing to look out to the sea, and in front of me was a bleached expanse of white crystals sparkling in the brilliant sun. As the chilly air whipped at us, I thought, "Snow on the beach!" I had never dreamed such a thing was possible. I wanted to run down onto the snow-covered sand, but before I could, Dad scooped me up and hustled us off the boards, back to the warmth and comfort of Tanty Anna's. When we got back, the scent of Tanty's delicious cooking greeted us. We warmed up with hot drinks and a scrumptious homemade lunch and then snuck away to play on our own while the grown-ups talked.

The Ariel Hotel was a wonderland for two city kids. The Ariel Hotel was magic itself. My Tanty Anna was a really strong woman. Her husband, a sickly man, had passed away before I was born. She ran that hotel with just the help of one other person, her childless niece. They had that in common; cousin Debbie was childless too. That's probably why we got so much love and attention whenever we came to the hotel. The only year-round support staff was a dual-duty cook/cleaning lady named Lovey. Lovey always had our back, covered our misdeeds and saved us the sweetest treats.

The hotel had only three floors of sleeping accommodations, and each floor had seven rooms. I guess that was manageable for three strong women.

Above: An original Ariel
Hotel postcard. *Courtesy of
Bo Pergamet.*

Right: Janet and Coleman
Robinson on the porch of
the Ariel Hotel. *Photo: David
Rosen.*

Whether it was or not, the work always seemed to get done well. Everything was always spick-and-span, and the food…the food was incredible.

In its heyday, those three women served thousands of meals, three a day to the Ariel's guests, and nothing came out of a box. Tanty and Lovey baked fresh bread every day and made their own yogurt and pickles in huge crockpots on the back porch. Of course, in summer, there were more people on the staff. My mom always remembered the handsome waiters, working their way through college and having a summer of fun at the same time. She was a teenager the summers that she worked at the Ariel, and I guess those college boys were a treat to her eyes.

In the winter months, when I was a kid, well before the arrival of casinos, the cold closed down most of the boardwalk businesses. The movie theater and some restaurants stayed open but not the fun toy stores and arcades. While we did get our first glimpse of snow on the beach, we stayed inside for most of that visit.

We really didn't need the boardwalk attractions to be entertained. For a seven- and eleven-year-old, fun was self-made. While the adults had their tea, visited and solved the problems of their grown-up world, we explored.

Downstairs were the bathhouse stalls, leftover from a time when you had to shower and dress before coming up into the lobby or even your own room. We searched the kitchen, where the tall, old-fashioned, wooden cabinets held all kinds of giant pots and pans, more china than we had ever thought possible and wonderful, delicious treats. The shore has a unique smell, a mix of salt air, aged wood and, sometimes, decaying sea life. The hotel was always spotless, but that aroma lingers in my memory. We hunted through every floor upstairs, in and out of each empty, closed-down, eerie hotel room, looking for possible hidden treasure.

Twenty-one hotel rooms made the best hide-and-seek playground ever—so good that when we couldn't find each other, we just gave up, shouted for each other and used the stripped-down beds as trampolines. We jumped and flopped around until we fell down laughing so hard and for so long that it hurt.

That day stands out in my memory, not just for the snow on the beach, not only for the warm, loving hugs and not merely for the wonderful food but because the grown-ups were so involved in conversation that no one asked where we were playing, and we got away with jumping on more than twenty defenseless beds.

On the way home, we got the news: Tanty Anna had sold the Ariel Hotel. That was our last visit there. Life for our family was changing. Snow had blanketed our seaside memories.

Chapter 6

THE ATLANTIC CITY BEACH

Leesa Toscano

Trudging along the pearly sand, I can see
layers of untouched patches of snow.
The beach is so beautiful, I know!
My toes wiggle in my shoes, slush against earth, leaving
deep impressions in the frozen covered sand.
The beach is beautiful…
Approaching the ocean, I smell a fishy odor in the air.
A frosty chill blows through my hair.
I cover my head with the hood of a coat and bury my
hands in pockets for warmth.
I focus my attention on the foaming, murky waves.
Ah! The ocean misbehaves. She rages against the shore,
sounds like a ferocious tiger's roar.
One reckless wave greets me by soaking my shoes.
The water, so frigid, penetrates through socks to my toes.
The Atlantic City beach is beautiful…
With euphoric eyes, I observe, what seems to be…
the whole sky peering down at me.
A multitude of bulging clouds hang down low.
The quarter moon appears from the south, so slow.
A white-and-gray seagull glides through the air and
swirls downward, screeching a thunderous cry.

A lone walk on the beach. *Leesa Toscano.*

Two seagulls and two pigeons appear, outstretching
their wings without fear. In silence,
they swoop and land on sand.
I quickly scamper toward the birds;
I lose my balance and slide on a sheet of ice.
I tumble downward onto earth's paradise.
The birds, at different intervals, soar into the sky.
Ah! My feathered friends, goodbye!
The Atlantic City beach is beautiful…
I lift myself off the ground.
A stroll along the seashore ends a perfect day.
And I, too, like the birds, must go on my way.

Chapter 7

A PALACE OF WISDOM

Bob Levin

ummers were a time for transformations, of which some were more complete than others. Like Chickie Grossinger's, who'd earned his nickname by being scared of everything from chalk dust to angry mutters but came back to ninth grade having been so successful with young ladies under the boardwalk that he had the strut of any DA'd, pegged-panted hood and had self-modified into the more swaggering "Chick."

Maybe it was the sun's heat that burnt away old skin. Maybe it was an expansion of the hardening that walking barefoot provided one's feet. (The goal then was to stamp out lit butts, like Herb Kepler, who lived in Margate year-round.) Maybe it was the absence of teachers tamping one's impulses down. Or maybe it was the presence of the Atlantic, stretching out forever, seemingly unbordered, unnarrowed, uncontrolled by red light or stop sign like West Philadelphia's streets. But it always felt, before leaves had started to fall, one was charged to begin anew.

When I was young, we spent summers at the shore. For the first month, my father would join my mother, brother and me on weekends. The second, he'd stay. The last of these summers was 1954, when I was twelve. We had a house on Buffalo Avenue in Ventnor, three blocks from the beach. It had a sandy backyard, a curbside tree with flowers I had never seen and boxes of *Reader's Digest* of the homeowners' accumulation, in which I read about "Most Unusual Characters" and "Life in These United States" and every murder I could find.

Dan Walsh and Sean Stack in jail at a boardwalk souvenir photo shop. *Courtesy of Sean Stack.*

I didn't know about Club Harlem then. I didn't know about White House hoagies or pizza at the Baltimore Grill or Tony Mart's across the causeway in Somers Point. I had not heard the rumors about the divorcées hanging like golden apples in the Ambi Lounge, waiting to be plucked. It was well before Labor Day weekends when two guys would rent a hotel room where six more would crash and when I once ended up so drunk on vodka and grape juice at a Harold Johnson fight at the Convention Center that I had to buy the next morning's *Inquirer* so I could tell my father how I'd liked it. And it was way before 1967, when Max Garden—whom I had not seen since fourth grade—and I celebrated his last summer before splitting for the coast by booking to AC and, stoned, tripped on Lucy the Elephant.

"Like, what if you went to sleep, and it was there, next door, the next morning?"

"Like what if a whole herd of them?"

"Like this whole elephant Levittown, man?"

But in 1954, drugs and drinking and divorcées were not within the range of contemplation. The other end of the Atlantic was easier to imagine. I had met characters, especially Max, who would prove "unforgettable" but were then only friends of whom, to varying degrees, my parents disapproved. For us, that summer's fun came from Skee-Ball and pokerino and riding waves on rubber rafts. Looking back, though, from the perspective of a sixty-year ascent into my future, I can see first steps taken toward what came.

Which brings me to Entertaining Comics—ECs.

They were—*Tales from the Crypt, Vault of Horror, Haunt of Fear, Crime* and *Shock SuspenStories, Weird Science* and *Weird Fantasy, Frontline Combat, Two-Fisted Tales* and *Mad*—like nothing else on the stands. Better written and better drawn. More sex and more violence. (Admittedly, at twelve, the violence

Feeding pigeons was a frequent pastime on the boardwalk. *Courtesy of Jill Moses.*

still held greater appeal.) They even, amid the gore and cleavage, held a progressive agenda: antiwar, pro-equality and pro–free speech, more than George Orwell.

This excellence was not universally recognized. Most of my classmates had no interest in comic books. My teachers thought my education would benefit from readings with greater spiritual uplift. My parents, concerned by articles in the press, forbade the purchase of anything "scary." And America's disapproval of the effect of comic books on juveniles in general would lead to a comic book code that would soon gut the field.

But Max dug ECs. So did Davie Pinsky and Fletcher Rabinowitz, other neighborhood kids, with whom we bonded over this passion. (Their parents drew no line like mine, and they opened their acquisitions to my viewing.) Another bond was that none of us were destined to captain football teams or date cheerleaders. (Fletcher, as it turned out, would have preferred dating football captains.) We did not, however, take our minority status as a negative. We *knew* ECs were the best. And our recognition that our peers and parents and teachers were wrong was a valuable lesson.

My transformation, while drabber than Chickie's, was as valid. It had rained the afternoon it happened. Swimming was out. The schoolyard held no softball game. I took off on my bike, heading straight until a signal changed my direction, a ritual I followed. Like I'd later hear, any path's a journey.

The street was one I'd not seen before. It was narrow, its houses shabby and crammed too close together, it seemed, for a breeze to blow between. On the Monopoly board, it would have been purple or, at best, orange. The beach lay at its end.

Midway down the block, a fellow, about eighteen, sat on an apple crate. A Camels pack peeked from the rolled sleeve of his T-shirt. A corkscrew of black hair spiraled down the middle of his forehead. Comic books spread around his feet led me forward like a Geiger counter's click. He lit a smoke with a one-thumbed flick of match against flint.

His stacks held Batmans and Supermans. They held ECs even my pals did not have. He had his eye on a motorcycle jacket and was liquidating for pennies on the dollar…er, dime. I left the Joker and Mr. Mxytplx for others. I piled a couple dozen ECs before me: axe murders and electrocutions, rotted corpses and zombies especially.

Then I explained my hesitation.

"I understand, kid, believe me, but what your folks donno won't hurcher. Y'understand what I'm saying?"

I said I couldn't lie to my parents.

"My point, exactly." He blew smoke over my shoulder. "Y'mind if I call you 'Kid'?"

I shook my head. I wanted to hear his thinking. And I wanted those comics. A rising tide exploded on the shore, echoing through the storm-clouded sky.

"Whachu ain't seeing is how you bein' screwed. A classic case of overkill, the forest hiding your trees."

I asked him to be more specific.

"I was just getting to that." He flicked ash from his cigarette. "Y'got to focus on the rule. The rule and nothin' but the rule. The rule draws the line."

"I can't buy scary comics." Sweat ran down my arms.

"And horror comics are scary." He pulled away *Haunt*, *Vault*, *Crypt*. I was sorry to see them go. "But don't look so sad. One good thing about lines, kid; by nature, they ain't wide." He slid *Frontline Combat* and *Two-Fisted* at me. "And war comics ain't horror. Am I right or am I wrong?"

"Yeah," I said. Flame throwers and saber charges and scalped Indians. I still had those.

"Iwo Jima," he said, tapping one issue. "Civil fucking War. You tell your folks, good as history lessons."

A greenhead fly had landed on my arm. I smashed it before it bit.

"And science fiction ain't horror. Science fiction's educational. That's why they call it 'science.'" On the cover of the topmost *Weird Fantasy*, a multitentacled, bug-eyed blob menaced a scantily clad, buxom blonde. He layered it beneath an issue on which a rocket ship chastely approached the moon. "Some of 'em got stories by famous author Ray Bradbury, to improve your mind."

I don't remember what he said about *Crime* and *Shock*, but I did not go home with them either.

When I returned to Buffalo Avenue, my heart pounded, and my voice cracked. I repeated for my parents everything I had heard about science and history and literature. I explained forests and trees. My parents offered less resistance than when, a few months earlier, I had sought permission to buy a horned toad.

"You should've bought them all," Max said, when I told him.

He kept dropping that on me, sometimes out of nowhere, sometimes years apart. "You should've bought them all, Bob," leaving a record hop. "You should've bought them all," pissing after a keg party. "Shoulda bought them all, man," snorting meth in the men's room at Pep's. Max did not believe in self-denial. He stood beside Blake on the roads of excess. For a long time, I could not slip that line's barb. It held me, most often, alone, at night, riding home from bars, lying in bed, not the ocean booming but something equally deep, equally threatening, equally eternal.

But a near half-century of work and luck shook it. Max OD'd. Davie suicided. Fletcher, I donno… AIDs? The meager load I carried off that muggy afternoon might have meant I remained too tightly leashed. Still… In "A Sound of Thunder," whose EC adaptation was in my bundle, Ray Bradbury demonstrated, through a character who returns from a trip back in time on which he accidentally squashed a butterfly to find that the liberal democracy he'd left has become a fascist state, that any act can alter a future. So, long content—and long marveling at this contentment—I hold more gratitude for the fellow who provided me a slight quanta of courage and duplicity, and for my folks, who acceded to it, than I resent myself for not having more fully embraced the forbidden.

Chapter 8

DRY CLEANING THE PAST:
ATLANTIC CITY TAILOR SHOP

Shelley Andress Cohen

I'm losing the threads of my history,
mending, always mending
Where did it begin?
With a tailor's chalk, a hard white square,
in the wrinkled hands of an old craftsman,
a tape measure around his neck
Weaving my way through musty smells
of dust and cobwebs enveloping
racks of unclaimed clothes
Faded signs advertise Invisible Weaving,
Sanitized Dry Cleaning,
Clothes Pressed While You Wait
Two old sewing machines littered with pins
bobbins humming inside
wheels purring in my mind
Bolts of fabrics lying
in the display window graveyard
sharing space with dead flies
Then the high counter where
the ancient cash register sits
The No Sale button opens the cash drawer
where quarters can be pilfered.

Shelley Cohen outside her grandfather's tailor shop. *Courtesy of Shelley Andress Cohen.*

There's a shelf with loose buttons, old ledgers,
the forgotten debris of daily living
But also, a brownspeckled,
flaking
notebook filled with foreign handwriting,
curlicues of thoughts never deciphered,
Cardboard postcards in faded hues
My unknown relatives speaking with their eyes
Their clothes, their stares state
they never escaped Russia

Added to the missing
a portrait of a heavybearded
patriarch
sheltered by a massive mahogany frame
props up the back door, unnoticed
Find me!
Beckons my great-grandfather
I wander to the wideopen
last room,
steamfilled
by a massive sweat box,
the pressing machine, next to it
on a brokendown
daybed
littered with magazines
I smell hard work's useless effort
A shelf on the wall
holds rows of browncorked
bottles
marked with skull and crossbones
dustcovered,
distilling future
diseases, this sepia monotony
Sews up the past

Chapter 9

MISS AMERICA BLOSSOMS

Janet Robinson Bodoff

At seven years old, the most glamorous thing I ever saw was Miss America contestants riding down the boardwalk dressed in sparkly outfits on the back of shiny new cars. As if that was not exciting enough, the cars were interspersed with floats covered by tons of beautiful flowers, glitter and streamers. I can still recall the scent of those floats festooned with what seemed like a million blooms. Mingled with the ocean breeze, it was pure perfume. Oh, how I wanted one of those flowers.

My first visit to the parade was magical, and returning to the parade is still as exciting to this grownup. When I was seven, my mom brought my little brother and me to the parade, as her mom had brought her. Like so many other little girls, we dreamed of fancy dresses, tiaras and unattainable beauty. We were not the first. Generations of little girls had the same dreams.

The pageant and its parade began in 1920 when local Atlantic City businessmen sought a way to make the summer season last past the Labor Day holiday weekend. They did it with a "Fall Frolic," a floral-decorated rolling chair parade peopled with bathing beauties. But there was no contest yet.

The following year, many East Coast newspapers sponsored contests to boost circulation, and the winners won a trip to Atlantic City to participate in the city's first beauty contest. Margaret Gorman won as "the Most Beautiful Bathing Girl in America" in 1921. Soon people began calling her "Miss America." By 1922, over fifty newspapers sent representatives to the contest;

A Miss America contestant shows off her shoes. *Photo: Ines Bloom.*

in 1923, seventy entrants arrived. The pageant missed a few years in the late 1920s but resumed in the 1930s and continues to this day.

For most families, the parade heralded the end of summer, back to the city and back to school. For those of us who lived here, it meant the beginning of the peaceful months when we had the boardwalk to ourselves. The pageant parade was always an exciting last hurrah to the summer.

Like a party on the boardwalk, the pageant and its parade have always been a huge draw, bringing hundreds of thousands of tourists to Atlantic City. In 2006, the contest moved to Las Vegas for five years, but it soon returned to its roots at the shore, and the 2014 Miss America was crowned back in Atlantic City.

With the return of the pageant came the return of the parade. The parade is always memorable, with beautiful floats provided by area businesses and marching bands from local and distant schools. Although the first parade was one of rolling chairs, floats pulled by local workers and lifeguards soon became the mainstay.

By the 1930s, many contestants glided down the boards in individual floats that were sponsored by various businesses. Piers, hotels, saltwater taffy shops and utilities, among others, sponsored dramatic and glamorous floats. The floats were always adorned with beautiful girls. Over the years, they dressed as fish, lobsters and southern belles with big hoopskirts and waved to the crowds from floats covered in sequins, feathers, flowers and crystals. In 1939, the Chicago World's Fair sent a spectacular bathing beauty–clad float down the parade route. By the 1950s, the girls traveled in the back of new and antique convertibles, as they still do to this day.

Every year, the public anxiously awaits the announcement of the parade marshal. Parade organizers have always endeavored to present the most appealing attraction possible. The marshal was always well known and chosen to add to the draw of the parade. Marshals included radio and TV personality Arthur Godfrey, Broadway star Carol Channing, singer Eddie Fisher and film actress Joan Crawford.

In 1952, the floats and beauties were led by parade marshal Marilyn Monroe. She was glamorous and at the height of her popularity, in town to promote a movie, and she graciously agreed to lead the parade. She drew huge crowds.

Crowds pack the boardwalk for the Miss America Parade. *Private collection.*

The parades of my childhood had all the flash and flourish that could dazzle a wide-eyed child. The entire mammoth production was a national effort, not the least of which came from citywide and statewide contests around the country, as well as a massive effort in Atlantic County.

Local preparations for the parade began months before the pageant. Volunteers helped out in so many ways. Young men acted as escorts to the contestants, and mature women were chaperones for the girls. Local volunteers helped build floats and acted as ushers and chauffeurs who drove the contestants around town and down the boardwalk.

If you were working for a business that had a float in the parade, there was a good chance that you could end up in the parade, waving at the crowds from your company's float. What fun it was to wave at your friends and neighbors as you cruised down the boardwalk in lavish style.

Antique car owners and car dealers throughout the area cleaned and shined convertibles to transport the pageant contestants. The bathing beauties rode on top of the back seat of a shiny convertible with their feet on the back seat and their shoes unseen as the crowds along the boardwalk yelled, "Show us your shoes." The girls always obliged. Over the years, their shoes and shoe embellishments got bigger and better. I remember seeing one Miss New York with skyscrapers growing up from her toes. Today the parade is called the "Show Us Your Shoes Parade."

The state beauties dressed in beautiful gowns or costumes that reflected their home states. One year, a contestant from Texas dressed as a cowgirl, and a girl from Hawaii wore a hula skirt and a lei.

The Miss American Pageant Parade was always before the contest's final judging on Saturday night, and I remember it taking place on Tuesday night when I was young and then on Friday night. The pageant had official viewing areas where you could buy a seat, and any business on the boardwalk that had room would set up folding chairs and sell the privilege to watch the parade from them. Families who didn't want to pay for seating brought their own places to sit.

Visitors would come hours before to set up their beach chairs along the boardwalk in between the paid seating areas. They brought food and drinks, blankets if a chilly evening was predicted or to spread at their feet for their kids to sit on. Some would lay a blanket right on the boards and put out a picnic for their friends or family; some would sit on the railing along the route. All of them yelled at the girls to turn and face them so that we could get a look at or snap a picture of their beautiful faces.

Lots of people got creative. Guys dragged lifeguard stands to the railing so that they could sit on top and see the parade. Anyone who could find a vantage point along the route was there. From the balconies of hotels like the Ambassador or the roofs of accessible buildings like Steel Pier, people crowded the parade route to get a glimpse of the beauties and pick out their favorite.

The parade came onto the boardwalk uptown on the wide ramp of Massachusetts Avenue. The porches along the street were packed with people getting the first look at the procession. We always watched the parade near Albany Avenue, another wide ramp at the end of the parade where the floats left the boardwalk.

Bands came from all over the country to participate. I can still recall the rhythmic beating of the drums and the blare of the horns as they passed us by. Patriotic songs and popular tunes preceded and followed the bathing beauties. For kids who vacationed in Atlantic City, marching in the parade was an honor to boast about when you got home. For those who watched, the bands enhanced and heightened the emotion of the evening.

Up and down the boardwalk, viewers were interacting with contestants. The parade would stop intermittently for bands to perform, and that would give kids an opportunity to run up to their favorite contestants and ask for autographs or give them a penny for good luck.

As my first visit to a Miss America Pageant Parade was ending, I got my opportunity. As the parade turned onto the ramp, a big, beautiful, flower-encrusted float stopped right in front of us. My mom said this was my chance. I got up my nerve and jumped up, ran up to the float and pulled off a big, fluffy, red flower. I slept with it under my pillow, and that night, I dreamed of Miss America Pageants to come.

Chapter 10

THE TASTE OF ATLANTIC CITY

Morgan Mulloy

The smell of bread
on Tennessee
is my home.

Those white- and blue-painted
cinder block walls
stand as the trunk
to my family tree.

I once had my name
on the bumper
of those trucks.
The one before the
back door was designed
to look propped open and
the panicked phone calls began.

The rye bread toasted
with a thin layer of butter
is my medicine,
and it wouldn't taste
as great, as memorable,
without that AC water.

Chapter 11

BOARDWALK

Gail Fishman Gerwin

We're on the boardwalk in Atlantic City,
my sister and I, she in her new mouton fur,
leopard trim around the wrists and collar,
I protected from November chill by a grey
wool coat from Ginsberg's in Passaic,
double row of large barrel buttons
down the front, a warm cloche hat
to cover my ears.

When I ask about our ages in the photo,
she tells me she's still in high school:
I'm sixteen or seventeen, she says.
She's seven years older, I'm seven years
younger—seven years younger for life.

A postcard from the Traymore Hotel at Park Place. *Private collection.*

Our mouths agape, we feed fat pigeons;
they flit above, skim our shoulders, cluster
on our hands to nip kernels bought at the stand
in the strip of open storefronts.
Behind us a pavilion's slanted roof, where the
emblem *Childs* in bold white script splashes
from eave to eave, beckons tourists to dine.

For years, our father drove the family
to Atlantic City for Thanksgiving,
to the Traymore Hotel at Illinois Avenue,
a majestic building with golden roof caps,
ocean views and, later, a glass-bottom
indoor pool, a luxury unknown back home.

I find this photo treasure in a fruitless
attempt to organize my home as birthdays
pass, as friends die, as growing grandchildren
grace our family. I scan it, sharpen edges,
but leave grooves of age that mar the image.
The young sisters, frozen statues in the center,
remain unscathed, captured by the parent
who holds the Kodak Brownie Box.

Eva, Janet and Coleman Robinson enjoy a relaxing
rolling chair ride along the boardwalk in the
summer of 1947. *Photo: David Rosen.*

Mother or father snaps us without a thought
toward the future, when they will rest together
under winter's hard earth, when they will
leave my sister, forever seven years older,
and me—still seven years younger for life,
to recall Novembers when we fed fat pigeons
on the boardwalk in Atlantic City.

Chapter 12

RHYTHMS OF AN ISLAND

Pat Hanahoe-Dosch

$\mathcal{I}$ grew up in a small town "down beach" from Atlantic City, on the same island. In those days, before casinos, the houses weren't as expensive as they are now, and much like the rest of the island, it was a family-oriented resort town. In those days, most summer residents were second-home owners, not renters, who came every year after school was out, spending the whole summer there until it was time to go back to school and their other home, but most of the neighborhoods were home to year-round locals, who continued to live there even after having to rebuild in some way after one storm or another. Hurricanes, nor'easters, storms came and went, but the locals stayed and loved our island. We learned to board up windows, keep candles and matches in drawers and ride out bad weather with respect but not fear. We knew where to evacuate to on the mainland, if necessary. Many chose to stay, usually, even for serious hurricanes like the storm of '62 or, later, Sandy. This was home. For years now, though, I have lived in other places, far from any large body of water. I have learned that for those of us lucky enough to grow up there, our island shapes us in ways that are hard to recognize until we find ourselves living in other places, far from the ocean.

Most of us on the island grew up playing on the beach in the summer, learning how to swim and be fearless, diving into the waves or surfing them with rafts, surfboards or just our bodies. My friends, siblings and I grew up knowing how to find interesting shells, how to dig for sand crabs and where to find large mussels, clams and sometimes even channeled whelks (that we called conch shells, though they aren't), which some locals cleaned and ate,

Above: Downbeach on Ventnor Avenue when trollies rode up and down the island. *Private collection*.

Left: Beach days frequently included building castles in the sand. *Photo: Janet Robinson Bodoff.*

steamed or barbecued. I learned to respect the ocean and not swim around the jetties or during rip tides, to look at the ocean and see when the currents were strong and what direction they were going in. I learned to identify a sand bar by the way the waves break before getting to the beach's edge. I could swim and hold my breath underwater not long after I'd learned to walk and, eventually, could gauge approximately how cold the water was just by how quickly my feet and legs did or didn't grow numb while wading through it. Even in the cold weather, as I grew older, I walked or jogged on the beach and learned to love the peace of a beach empty of people, the joy in sharing the sand cushioning my stride with just gulls and sandpipers for company, the bits of shells crunching under my feet, the briny wind and spindrift swirling up from the waves.

The ocean is such a dominant force in the lives of islanders that its tides and rhythms become ours. Driving over the causeway to the bridge, and then home, from school or other business, I could always immediately tell the level of the tide and whether there would probably be flooding in certain areas if the moon was full and there had been a lot of rain. Would there be a lot of waves? Good surfing? Good fishing? Would there be a lot of clams or seaweed scattered at the wrack line? Would the air smell of them at low tide? I never thought of that as a fetid stink. It was just the natural smell of the ocean's detritus. Would the lower areas in town flood? The tides determined the best time of day to walk on the beach or go swimming in the summer. Certain streets always flooded a bit at high tide in certain kinds of weather, especially on the beach blocks and the streets back by the bay. Those were the streets always hit worst in a storm. Our house was on a beach block, but it was also one of the highest points on the island, so though the water would come up the street and flood the sides of it, our house and those around us were usually safe, though our basement sometimes flooded. Most houses on the island don't have basements for that reason, but we loved ours because we had a shower down there where we could wash and change after coming back from the beach and not track sand through the house.

My orientation to the rest of the world was determined by where the ocean lay. The sun rose over the ocean, and home was always east. The Pine Barrens, and then Philadelphia, were always west of the ocean. The whole world was somewhere west, south or north of the island, which was the center of the world. This seemed like a fundamental fact of life. When I left the island to live in other places, I found it hard to determine directions wherever I was. My inner compass still works best only when I am home, visiting my parents on the island.

In high school, which was on the mainland in the city of Absecon, I met many classmates who were not from one of the islands. The Catholic school to which my parents sent my siblings and me served families in a large area of islands and the mainland. I was sure the students from mainland areas envied those of us who came from the islands. I tried to be kind and not talk about the beach to them. Some had been to the beach only a few times in their lives, though they lived only a half hour's drive or so from one of the islands. I couldn't imagine living like that. Later, I attended the Richard Stockton State College of New Jersey, which is located in the Pine Barrens, on the mainland but close enough that I could commute from home. Many of my fellow students were from towns scattered throughout New Jersey, including the Pine Barrens, or places further north or southwest. I pitied them. How sad to live in a landlocked place like Vineland or, worse, a large, landlocked city like Camden, Philadelphia or Newark. What did people do in the summer if they couldn't go to the beach? How terrible to breathe air that didn't have the smell of the ocean. I did love the smell of the Jersey pitch pines that surrounded our college campus and still do as I drive down the Black Horse Pike when I return home. But I have always been grateful to reach the causeway and drive through the marshes to the bridge. It became a lifelong ritual to roll down the car window and breathe in the salt air as soon as I turned off Tilton Road onto the Margate Bridge Causeway.

When I moved to Tucson, Arizona, to attend graduate school, I was lost, though I loved the Sonoran Desert. I loved the mountains that seemed to provide borders by surrounding the city in a protective loop. Tucson was small enough then that it was more of a town than a city, so there wasn't much pollution, and it was pretty. The architecture was different from what I was used to, and I could drive straight down Speedway Boulevard into the mountains and the saguaro forest, where there were very few houses or people, just great hiking and beautiful views of the desert, mountains and a sky the deep blue that comes from no moisture in the air. The sunsets were colorful and gorgeous because of the sand and dust, but the dry air was harsh and acrid. It burned my sinuses, and the sand and dust in the air made me cough; it took months for me to orient myself by which mountains the sun rose and set over. Driving through flat sections of the desert outside the city at night, I imagined I was passing over the salt marshes of home. The flat ground was dark, but in the distance, the lights of the city stretched, like an island in the distance.

After graduate school, I moved to San Diego, thinking I could find a job in such a big city and live by the ocean, but my sense of direction was completely turned around. Now the sun set over the ocean, and the water was west, not east. And I couldn't afford to live on one of the islands there. I had to live further east in the cheaper areas, in the California desert, which has its own beauty but not the lush, sometimes surreal landscapes of the Sonoran Desert. I had to drive long distances and battle bad traffic to get to one of the beaches and the ocean. But it was always worth it. I felt like I was home, until the sun began to set over the water. That was always disorienting. And the Pacific Ocean is not the same as the Atlantic. It is colder in summer, bluer, with larger waves but calmer on most days. Its moods are not as seasonal. The Atlantic in winter is wild, harsh and unforgiving. The area off the northeast coast is called Shipwreck Alley because it is so rough that it has become home to many wrecks over the centuries, even in modern times. The Pacific does not have the same gray and dark, cloudy green colors. To me, the currents don't seem as strong, as urgent, as compelling.

I have lived all over the world in pursuit of my career, mostly in landlocked locations. Perhaps the hardest loss to acclimate to in all of these places has been the absence of the sounds of the surf.

The sounds of the waves breaking on sand and jetties, of tides flowing in and out, were always in the background when I was on the island. Sometimes the surf was extremely loud if a storm was approaching or leaving. When those sounds became too loud, they could stir up fear or excitement. The waves sometimes roared and threw themselves at the shoreline in a frenzy of wind and currents. Or on calm nights, they lapped at the sand and called in a soft, varied rhythm, like some wild force momentarily tamed, singing softly. At night, especially in summer when my windows were open, the surf lulled me to sleep. Those were the sounds of the familiar edges of my world, of the ocean whose moods and storms literally and figuratively shaped and reshaped the world around me, the sounds of the borders that defined what was safe and what was not, where I could go and where I could not. I could not sleep without those sounds.

For a long time, in order to sleep, I had to pretend that the sounds of traffic outside my window were the sounds of the surf and tides. Now I live on a quiet, suburban street in Pennsylvania. There isn't much traffic here at night, but in summer I hear a grand orchestra of insects and frogs outside my window, along with the occasional cat fight and birds. In the winter, the only sounds are the ticking of the clock on my bureau, the groans and whines of my refrigerator and the occasional hissing of my hot water heater. Sleep is still hard. The silence is sometimes terrifying.

Chapter 13

THE INVASION

Janet Robinson Bodoff

They're here!

The invasion has begun.
Our roads are clogged with them.

They have arrived in force.
Vehicles loaded with provisions.
Armed for this incursion.

They outnumber us.
Their forces are rolling in,
spreading across our land.

The invasion has begun.

They have arrived at our doorstep.
Bicycles strapped to the back of
    their cars.
Luggage lashed to their roofs.

The invasion has begun.

By tomorrow they will gather their
    troops.
They will storm our quiet, peaceful
    beaches
armed with multicolored chairs,
    umbrellas and heavily packed, icy
    coolers.

At the beach with multicolored chairs and umbrellas. *Photo: Janet Robinson Bodoff.*

Fourth of July fireworks. *Photo: Janet Robinson Bodoff.*

They will amass their front on our
  sandy, shell-strewn shores.
Marching along with rubber rafts
  and boogie boards in hand.
The small are ones pushing
  forward, dragging buckets and
  shovels behind them.

The invasion has begun.

Their weapons are aimed at
Our sea life,
Wildlife,
Nightlife,
Lifestyle.

Peace and solitude has left our fair
  land.
Fourth of July weekend
has arrived at the Jersey shore.

Chapter 14

HI-HAT JOES: TEENAGE HEAVEN

Janet Robinson Bodoff

*I*n a city filled with attractions designed to lure visitors, it was the number one drawing card for us. In the 1950s and '60s, Hi-Hat Joe's was the epicenter of teenage fun in Atlantic City, New Jersey. Located between Montpelier and Chelsea Avenues on the boardwalk, it was a magnet for teenagers. One of many little storefront businesses that lined the boardwalk, it was just a small lunch counter, but it drew thousands of kids to its door for a burger, a mug of birch beer from the tap or just to be there. Joe's was *the* place to hang out if you were between thirteen and nineteen, although it was mostly Jewish high school kids who couldn't stay away.

Their names were Rubin and Rosen, Goldberg and Greenfield, Schwartz and Stein, Fishman and Feingold. Chelsea Beach was the most popular gathering place by the sea for families from surrounding Jewish communities from north, south and west, and Joe's was where you could find their teenage children.

I was one of them, the kids who made more fun of their time at the shore than anyone had a right to. From morning to night, it was Chelsea Beach and Hi-Hat Joe's.

Every summer, Atlantic City would flood with families coming to enjoy the beach and the boardwalk for a day, a week or the summer. If those families had teenagers, often their kids wouldn't wait for summer. On the first warm days of spring, many of us would cut school and make our way to the shore. Some, tempted by the ocean, would wade or jump all the way in,

Left: The Hi-Hat Joe's logo. *Private collection.*

Below: Some of the many arcade pinball machines that dotted the boardwalk for years. *Bernard Jenkins.*

fully clothed. After all, you could always lie in the sun and dry off. Some, I'm told, borrowed scissors from Hi-Hat Joe's to turn their pants into cut-offs just to take a swim. Others would frequent the nearby arcades with their pinball and Skee-Ball machines. Even if we were there for only an hour or two, we'd all be sure to stop at Joe's.

At any time of day, kids would congregate en masse in front of our gathering place on the boardwalk or on the beach. The boardwalk between Montpelier and Morris Avenues was teenage real estate from Memorial Day to Labor Day when we had to get back home for school.

On any given summer morning during legal biking hours, from seven to ten o'clock, the boardwalk would be mobbed with people. There were always

Teenagers crowded Chelsea Beach in the early 1960s. Chelsea Beach was a teen mecca from the 1940s to the 1970s. *Photo: David Kieserman.*

groups of bicycles parked in front of Hi-Hat Joe's. Kids and adults out for some fresh air and exercise would stop for a glass of fresh-squeezed orange juice, a specialty of the house, and perhaps a bagel with "a schmear"—a thick coating of cream cheese.

This ritual would often include making plans for the evening or the weekend. Those plans always included the beach, showering, dressing up and then coming back to Hi-Hat Joe's to hang all evening on the boardwalk.

At lunchtime you could run up from the beach and get a burger or a hot dog, a frozen banana and an ice-cold mug of draft birch beer. The beach was always so crowed with umbrellas, chairs and peoples' blankets that they were often touching, and you had to try to tiptoe between them, burning your feet as you navigated the fiery sand until you got to your own clique. The sound of bongo drums keeping time, pulsing, with the waves, seemed to always be a backdrop to the amusement. Dotted on the blankets were kids holding aluminum reflectors under their chins, trying to speed up and enhance a tan to take back to the city. And, always, there was the smell of salt air mixed with baby oil and iodine or coconut suntan lotion.

If we wanted to swim and the ocean was plagued with jellyfish or tar, we went pool hopping—that is, sneaking into some of the better pools at some of the numerous hotels and motels in the area. Within a few blocks of Joe's, there were many to choose from: the Aloha, the Pageant and the

Ascot, among dozens more. The Ambassador pool was inside and not too easy to conquer, but the LaConcha was another story. Right there on the boardwalk, the indoor/outdoor pool was a snap to crash, especially if you were a cute girl or had a buddy who was a pool boy who would slip you one of the bright red wrist tags that showed you belonged in the pool. The Strand was easy to crash if you got there early for a swim, and many, many other pools were available to wily, persistent teens.

At night, the crowds were so big that people and rolling chairs had to inch their way through the throng. Every night, you could hear the rolling chair drivers yelling, "Watch the chair, please!" Teens would be everywhere, standing in the pathways, sitting on the railings or sneaking into an empty rolling chair that was strapped to the railings waiting for its rightful users (those who had paid for the chair) to arrive and chase them away. Finding an empty spot to sit on or stand by the railings that protected strollers from falling down onto the beach was ever a challenge. If you found a spot, you usually stayed there all evening, because if you did move, the spot would be gone before you could turn around. The police were always trying to make room for people to walk by. When pressed, we would move around a little, only to go right back after the cops left.

Most nights after dinner, dessert was purchased at a nearby candy store. We would choose from a molasses paddle or saltwater taffy at Steele's or Fralinger's, a Kohr Bros. soft-serve cone or a stop at A.L. Roth's Candy Store to get "polly" (sunflower) seeds and then go find an empty rolling chair, eat and spit the shells on the boards.

Everyone got really dressed up. Going out to dinner and strolling the boards was such a big deal, men would wear suits and women would wear

Ladies chat away the evening on rented rolling chairs that were lined up just past Hi-Hat Joe's. *Photo: Merill Kelem.*

their furs against an evening breeze; even us kids wore our best outfits. And those of us who wore high heels had to buy metal-lined plastic caps for our shoes so that our heels wouldn't get caught between the boards. You could always see men whose girls didn't have those protective caps, bent over pulling some lady's heel out from between the boards before they could move on.

There were lots of characters at Chelsea Beach. Boys who thought they owned the beach and boardwalk were often throwing their weight around, trying to impress girls and get other boys to do their bidding. I remember hearing about one guy who was bragging about working using some other guy's social security number. And there was the guy who introduced himself with: "I'm Wild Bill from Chestnut Hill. I never worked, and I never will." Maybe he didn't have a job, but he always had a hustle.

It was a free-for-all fun time where pranks were regularly pulled. Kids drove cars onto the boardwalk, trying not to get caught, just so they could say they did it. More times than most can remember, the fountain and the pool at the Deauville Hotel next to Hi-Hat Joe's would be secretively treated to a mysterious dose of soap that would turn it into an unwanted bubble bath. On Labor Day weekend in 1969, a full-sized boat somehow made it into the Deauville pool!

Lots of nasty tricks were committed. Once, an unfortunately hirsute teenage boy was given a bottle of suntan lotion to use; regrettably, the bottle was filled with Nair hair remover. After much peer pressure, he rubbed it into his chest and came away with handfuls of his hair. Further proof that kids can be mean. But it was all in enthusiastic, screwball good fun.

We came with our parents and stayed at one of the many rooming houses, hotels or motels that filled the town. Finally, and if we could convince our parents that we would be safe, we were allowed to rent a room with friends. We shared the cost with as many of us as we could fit in a room. We stayed up late and fell into bed in the wee hours of the morning. In most of those shared rooms, the actual renters woke up to the floors and bathtubs filled with kids who didn't have the price of a place.

There were lots of reasons to go to Chelsea, but for most of the kids who hung there, it was most important to meet other teens. It was the place to see and be seen. For blocks, there were boys looking for girls and girls looking for boys. Many of us found our first loves there.

The summer I was sixteen, I worked at Hi-Hat Joe's, serving fresh-squeezed orange juice and sliding around on the floorboards behind the counter. Working there wasn't really a difficult job—it was fun. Over the years, several people were proprietors of Hi-Hat Joe's, but in the late '50s and early '60s, the owner was Courtney Leiberman. In our eyes, he was the "old" man who owned the place. Of course, he was probably younger than many of us who gathered there are now. I remember him as a nice man. When we were required to work until closing, which sometimes was well past midnight, he would give those who needed it a ride home. Of course, some of us would accept the ride like polite kids, arrive home and then turn around and go back out again. There was always more fun to be had, no matter the hour.

For so many of us, those memories, that time and place, are such a genuinely important piece of our personal history. Fourteen or sixteen, boy or girl, with our parents or on our own, we all came of age at Hi-Hat Joe's on the boardwalk in Atlantic City.

Chapter 15

SEVENTEEN AND KISSED
AT THE STEEL PIER

Lucy Jerue

My claim to fame is that I was kissed by one of the Four Seasons. No, it was not Frankie Valli. It was Joe Long, the bass player.

I was the summer of 1968. My friends and I were all on the verge of getting our driver's licenses. But what good would that do us? Not one of us was going to be allowed to borrow the family car and drive from our hometown of Hammonton to Atlantic City. No matter. That wasn't going to stop us from getting there.

There was an NJ Transit bus that made runs from Philadelphia to Atlantic City. It stopped in Hammonton, the halfway point. We loved taking the bus because it gave us the independence to go to Atlantic City for the day and not have to depend on anyone's parents or family car. We were going to do this on our own terms.

I boarded the bus at Dan's Stationery Store with three of my friends. The bus brought us to the bus station in Atlantic City, and we walked the short distance to the boardwalk. As we approached the walk, I marveled at the salt air aroma, the throngs of people and the mix of junk food stands and souvenir shops.

We always loved to eat at a steakhouse on the boardwalk. I cannot recall the name. But, it was on the ocean side of the boardwalk. I know that I identified the location of this place a few years ago. I think half of it is now a shop that sells silky blouses and colorful skirts. I am not sure what became of the other half.

After our meal, we headed straight to the Steel Pier. What a place! Seeing the marquee was always a thrill. The headliners that day were Frankie Valli and the Four Seasons. That's why we were there.

There were plenty of other acts and attractions to see as well. There was the Al Albert's Showcase. This was a beauty and talent contest for little girls. They dressed up and showed their unique talents. It was cute at the time. Any feminist would see it as otherwise, no doubt. But remember, this was 1968.

There were movies also at the Steel Pier. You got this giant schedule to keep you on track for the day. You could see movies and live shows. You could enjoy the rides or go down to the depths of the ocean in the diving bell. In all my trips on the diving bell, I never saw any fish. But one could always hope. It's like Charlie Brown hoping to kick that football. Still, it was fun to travel to the ocean floor, fish or no fish.

If you knew about the Steel Pier, you knew about the diving horse. That was never a highlight for me personally. But I knew it was iconic and unique to the Steel Pier. I often felt sorry for that poor horse, having to jump down into the water. Even as a teenager, I knew this did not come naturally to a horse. I wondered if the trainer/rider was able to allay his fears.

My friends and I checked our Steel Pier schedules carefully to make sure we did not miss the Four Seasons. We arrived at their theater right on time to hear them entertain us. Valli sang all our favorites: "Big Girls Don't Cry," "Walk Like a Man," "Sherry," "Rag Doll." I could go on and on. We were loving every song and singing along. We wished the concert would never end. When it did end, after at least one curtain call, we were in love with the Four Seasons.

Being the clever geniuses that we were, we went to the back part of the

Starring acts light up the night. *Courtesy of Lucy Jerue.*

pier to see if we could figure out where their dressing room might be. We were on the boardwalk area at the back end of the pier. We were pretty sure we were in the right place. I have no idea why we stayed and hung around there. There were no other people back there.

Then it happened. Three of the Four Seasons came out. I think one or two of them lit up a cigarette. We spoke to them just like they were our big brothers. They were so friendly and down-to-earth. When they said goodbye to us, Joe Long, the bass player, leaned over and kissed each of us. We were in awe and completely starstruck. As I recall, we were walking in a goofy, happy daze as we walked away from the back of the dressing room area.

Now, you know that bus from Hammonton to Atlantic City ran again the next day. Of course, we were on it. Yes, we went once again to the Steel Pier. We were there for that Four Seasons concert. We went back to the dressing room area to look for Joe. He never came out. No one did. But it was okay. We were still starstruck, and we still loved the Four Seasons.

We would return to the Steel Pier many times. It was always fun to board the bus and be transported to that magical place.

Chapter 16

SUBMARINE RACES

Shelley Andress Cohen

This craggy tip of island was called
  the Point
just jetties, sea and a sandy space
short as my time of innocence
when I first heard about the
  submarine races
I was fourteen and learning, he was
seventeen and knowing
We went to the movies and then he
  drove here
to show me the submarines, me
  looking out,
he moving in and laughing when I
  told him
I saw nothing, but soon I saw the
  other parked cars
Inside each were heads hooked
  together,
the darkness hid what was
  happening deep inside,

the stealthy advances,
the silent trawlings
Suddenly, the squad car showed up,
  bright lights
scattering each car away, but who
  knows
how many submarines rose to the
  surface
nine months later, how many of
  those searchers
still remember the darkness of sea
  night,
the breaking sound of waves
I stand at the end of the jetty
  watching a
blinding red globe illuminate the
  bridge
till the fathomless night
slowly settles in

A great spot to watch the submarine races. *Photo: Leesa Toscano.*

Chapter 17

ATLANTIC CITY LUCK

Enid Shomer

I've been sitting on the boardwalk
all morning, watching the tourists
hurry toward their luck
and recalling the weekend I spent
here with Grandpa thirty years back.
He smoked Havanas, filling our room
with blue haze and talk.
The waiters, migrants from Brooklyn
for the season, spoke a New York
Yiddish even I could understand.

There were no casinos then, only
the sea dealing out its endless deck
of waves and the spectacle of the diving horse,
a chestnut in waterproof fringe and tack
who hourly plunged from the pier.

When Grandpa dozed under a striped
umbrella, I ventured out. The sea
was battleship grey, cold for July.
Whitecaps flecked with shell and grit

stung my skin. *Dangerous undertow.*
Submerged jetty. Beyond the breakers
the water was calm as broth. I swam out,
behind me the horse gathering speed
for another dive.

Then the current sucked me under—
a cold stream that wrapped my ankles
and waist. Drowning. This is what
lies between risk and luck: one gasp.
And the horse crashing again and again,
the saddle of sun on his back as he swam,
I astride him, his rough hide
between my legs, sour water
dripping from his mane.

I do not know how long he dived
after the hotels weathered to slums
and Grandpa yellowed from liver disease.
Or how I managed to surface again,
the beach, the striped umbrella
blinking into view, the horse
standing slack in the sun.
I think the ocean simply let me go,
buoyant but broken.

The diving horse performed multiple shows every day. *Private collection.*

Chapter 18

THE WAY BACK TO SHELTER I: CODE BLUE

Richard K. Weems

AUTHOR'S NOTE: Cities along the East Coast and well inland sweep their streets of homeless people and give them a one-way ticket to America's Playground, Atlantic City. Police sweeps along the beach intended to move homeless people from under the boardwalk have found whole residences that include mattresses, a variety of furniture pieces, TVs and hooked-up cable service. Often the sweeps gather people and send them to the Atlantic City Mission for shelter. Staff social workers try to help these individuals access the social services that they need. Richard K. Weems, a social worker there, worked with the two women who inspired the following stories.

She does not cry when she says she's going to kill herself

and the baby inside her. No fits, no rage,

no sincerity, but as her caseworker I have to cover my ass

and bring her to the ER, this girl I don't want so much to fuck

as know that she wants to be fucked, fucked

by every male counselor, her boyfriend's brothers,

and each guy she makes eyes at through the passenger window
on the way to the hospital. She traces the outline

of her belly as though that mound were a trophy,

proof that she can capture a man and make him

docile, though she's only here now, saying

what's she's saying, because her boyfriend hit her,

which he did because this is probably not his baby

and she has told him so. The boyfriend is a kung fu movie fanatic,

only hits girls, and has been expelled for the night.

The nurse, the doctor: no one

believes her, but she's going to be observed

overnight anyway, because she keeps on

making her claim, playing her shit hand since she has too much

invested in the pot to muck her cards. Luckily for her,

she'll be picked up

in the morning by a different counselor, who'll know

the situation, but not how poorly she played

her bluff. She can feign dignity, beg a little sympathy.

In the meantime, she'll sit in a harmless room

while I take the van back to the shelter. I should have been off

at eleven, and now the sky is a back-lit blue. Graveyard
is such a misnomer for this shift. It is, rather,

Moon over the ocean. *Photo: Janet Robinson Bodoff.*

code blue—life on the verge to somewhere else. An aging whore

in a jogging suit, looking to get in a trick or two

before quitting, whoops at each passing car.

Chapter 19

THE WAY BACK TO SHELTER 2:
TALKING WITH ANGELS

Richard K. Weems

Iris's schizophrenia had convinced her dad to take the side

of the uncle who had molested her,

and when the day counselor left me her months-empty bottle

of haloperidol, I felt as yellow and sickly as that white-capped plastic

about a late-night drive to the hospital.

As we passed Florida Ave., Iris told me about the angels

that were giving her advice on what job to take,

which boy to ask out, what toothpaste works best. I fudged

when she asked me, finally, if I also had angels.

I counted on divine powers to guide me safely

through Atlantic City traffic, so I admitted to a deity

in denominationally vague rhetoric—

my own little faith-based initiative.

Chemically deficient Iris smiled as though at an unwanted gift,

and I felt the segue for truth roll away under the van.

No angels had stopped her sick fuck of an uncle,

or the father she never mentioned if she could help it.

Those weren't angels she screamed for

before doctors found her proper dosage, when she'd run out naked

into the street. She was only religious

because she'd exhausted all other hope.

Iris told me how pretty the lights were on the Bally's building.

Only now, after having been run through injustice like a grinder,

could she see fairy wings on those lights.

Atlantic Avenue at night. *Private collection.*

Chapter 20

THE HOTEL ON ST. JAMES PLACE

Molly Golubcow

As the owner of a small hotel frequented by lost beings who had a little bit of money and a police record or two, my father sat behind the front desk of the Seacrest Hotel in Atlantic City in the early 1970s. It had been over twenty-five years since Hitler shot his prized shepherd and Ava drank some poison and Russian boots stomped over Berlin.

For my father, Atlantic City was not a desired or direct route from Miory, Poland. It began for him in 1942 as his ghetto was being liquidated. Told by the Nazis to go outside and be "counted" yet again, the 220 ghetto-dwellers were herded out to an open field. They were ordered to undress, line up— *schnell.* My father survived because of the word *God.* When the future of these naked humiliated souls became clear to him, my father cried out, "*Mein Gott.*" His prayer was immediately answered with a rifle butt to the left side of his head and one of Hitler Youth's finest yelling, "You have no God, he's ours." My father fell to the ground as the bullets began—old, young, good and even bad souls went up to heaven en masse.

My father lay unconscious until nightfall. When he awoke, nothing was moving. Even the blood had stopped flowing and covered the dead in a layer of blackened red crust. He staggered into the dark woods near the mass grave where he never before imagined himself spending a night. His entire family, part of the exodus direct to heaven that afternoon, left him alive and behind. He spent the rest of the war in those woods with a band of partisans, imagining the voice of his eight-year-old son calling him Tateh.

Left: Harry Golubcow looks out onto St. James Place. *Courtesy of Molly Golubcow.*

Right: Seacrest Hotel postcard. *Courtesy of Molly Golubcow.*

After the war, my father remarried and immigrated to America. He tried to find a life for his new family—first a chicken farm in Vineland and then the Seacrest Hotel. When I was eleven, the hotel in the middle of Atlantic City was our family business. There were boardwalk arcades clanging with the sounds of pinball machines and Skee-Ball, the Italian ice vendor pawning his wares on Million Dollar Pier, penny auctions with a shill planted in the third row, Kohr's custard swirled in chocolate/vanilla braids, miniature golf courses, the Belgium waffle man, Mr. Peanut giving away plastic bank replicas of himself and fortune-tellers who couldn't read a word in a newspaper but were scholarly with a palm if it held a five-dollar bill. On the corner of St. James Place and the Boardwalk, the neon sign advertising the Seacrest Hotel could be seen halfway down the block with the *L* flashing and hissing throughout the night.

My father sat behind the front desk, always ready to check in a customer. Hundreds of people would pass by his desk every summer. Some arrived with enthusiasm but left with disappointment—a child that would not get off the streets and come home, an alcoholic who could not give up his bottle, a husband and wife who gave up trying to make their marriage work. Others were down so low when they checked in, the Seacrest became their haven. Yvonne was one of those souls selling herself every night on Pacific Avenue so she could supply her needle with sweet liquid to soothe her veins. Smitty was her pimp.

One day, she decided to stop. I remember that morning waking up to a woman's desperate screams and trying to figure out if it was a dream. It was too bright out to be night and still too dark to be morning. It was the time when Yvonne handed over her earnings to Smitty. After a crashing noise, there was the sound of a hand slapping against a face and then another scream. The sounds were coming from the lobby. I knew my father was out there, so I bolted out of bed and ran toward the screaming.

The green ceramic lamp with the flower cutout lampshade was shattered on the floor. Yvonne's belongings were strewn out of her pocketbook on the floor by the front desk. "Stop it, you're hurting her." My mother was already there and pleading with Smitty to stop strangling Yvonne. My father kept yelling out Smitty's name, trying to jog some kind of humanity within him. But Yvonne's pink plastic earrings, like Christmas balls, swung back and forth with each squeeze of her neck and banged against Smitty's pinkie ring, a large gold S in a circle of diamonds. His strong hands, muscles tensed with a mission, were wrapped around Yvonne's neck as she gasped for air. Like a tango dip, her body was bent backward in a slight curve. If it weren't for the fact that Smitty was killing Yvonne, the pose would have seemed choreographed.

I remembered the first time I saw Smitty and Yvonne. They checked into room 29 as Mr. and Mrs. Smith, rarely speaking a word to each other. After checking in, Yvonne sat on the couch in the lobby eating crème-filled Tastykakes while watching cartoons on television. She was a dark-skinned Black woman, very thin, and she wore lots of makeup. Smitty went to make a call in the spray-painted gold phone booth in the lobby. He slowly walked toward the phone with a gait that came from life on the streets. He carefully closed the folding door in the booth. I was reading a magazine in the lounge chair next to the phone booth. Even though the sound was muffled, I could hear every word he said. Most of the conversation consisted of "A-ha," "Nah" and an occasional grunt. The only full sentence I heard him say was, "Look, I killed before, and I ain't got no problem killin' again." I wasn't exactly surprised. He looked the part of a B-movie pimp, and I knew to keep my life out of his. It came with the territory at the hotel—live and let live.

Smitty punctually paid his weekly rent in cash with money that Yvonne earned for him. He'd ask my father how business was going, my father would reciprocate and ask about his and they'd exchange a word or two about the weather. It wasn't that my father approved of Smitty's work, but for some reason, they understood each other. They'd both learned that life can throw people together and keep them together because of unusual reasons, whether it's in an alley, on a bus or in a marriage—anywhere. "Hitler was a strange matchmaker," my father would always comment about the new life and world he was thrust into.

Yvonne's face was streaked with a tears-and-mascara blend. My father kept shouting Smitty's name. A short, stocky man, my father looked dwarfed next to Smitty's long, angry body. *Here we go again,* my father must have thought, *tears and screaming and monsters killing in front of me again. I thought this was 1972; the Nazis were destroyed. But, here I am with demons before me.* Again, my father yelled Smitty's name and pleaded, "Smitty, it's not nice to do this in a lobby. Go to your room and do this."

It was a surreal moment. Was my father joking? This was not the time for humor. Was he concerned that a strangled woman in the lobby would be bad for business? This was not the time to think of business. It seemed to take hours for that sentence to translate into all of our minds. You could almost see Smitty digesting the words as he ever so slowly turned and looked at my father with a completely puzzled look on his sweaty face. In that split second, Yvonne broke away, and my mother whisked her behind the front desk. My father pushed Smitty outside, and it was all over. He saved someone from being killed, something my father could not do years before, even for his own family. Perhaps he was due a win. Perhaps it was more of a lucky day for Yvonne than a win for my father. Later that day, a man who looked like he could have been Yvonne's father took her away.

Smitty lived at the Seacrest until the end of the summer. A year later, we saw him again. It was Yom Kippur, the Day of Atonement, when God seals our fate in the book of life for another year. Who shall live and who shall die? It was a long day, and we were eager to get home and break the fast. As we exited the massive doors of Rodef Shalom synagogue on Pacific Avenue, Smitty happened to walk by. He ran over and shook hands with my father.

"How's business?" my father asked him.

They chatted for a few minutes. An Atlantic City policeman, directing traffic, stared at them, trying to figure out how these two men could have ever known each other. Smitty patted my father on the back and wished him well. My family went back to the hotel as Smitty walked down the street and turned into a bar. My father was right; Hitler was a strange matchmaker.

Chapter 21

LOST AND FOUND
IN ATLANTIC CITY

Sandy Warren

*W*hen I cautiously stepped off the bus in Atlantic City that crisp, early October afternoon in 1973, I had three pieces of baggage: a small case with a few clothes, two Gaines-Burgers and a leash; a tan wicker carrier holding my beloved, mangy old black-and-white cocker spaniel, Freckles; and the enormous, weighty mental baggage I was carrying around in my head.

I had been living in New York with my lover, jazz drummer Art Blakey, who divided his time between me and his third wife, Atsuko. Things turned to shit fast when he didn't have enough money to pay the rent at the Roger Williams Hotel and buy his heroin. So he did what any true junkie would do. He skipped the rent and copped the heroin. The manager quickly plugged the lock to our room, number 1406. Art conveniently plopped his ass down at Atsuko's, and I ended up on the street with twenty-five dollars in my bag. His hold on me was so great, I knew the only way I could break it and survive was to get outta town and not let him or his runnin' buddies know where I was. I had given up everything to be with Art, and now I needed to give up everything to be free of him.

I was counting on Atlantic City to help me unlock the emotional handcuffs and shackles I'd willingly submitted to and, if I wasn't asking too much, to help me find a bed and hot plate. I wasn't a religious person, but this is what I prayed for. After all, Atlantic City was the queen of resorts. She'd found a way, legal or otherwise, to help a lot of people down on their luck. Maybe I'd be next.

As I headed over toward Pacific Avenue and the boardwalk, I heard voices singing. Whether they were voices in my head or were coming from one of the buildings, I don't know. It doesn't matter. But this is what I heard: "Amazing grace! How sweet the sound that saved a wretch like me! I once was lost and now am found; was blind, but now I see."

The healing had begun. God was gonna share some grace with me, and it was gonna happen right here, starting right now. I checked into one of those '50s motels on Pacific Avenue somewhere between Iowa and Montpelier. It was steps away from the boardwalk and was equipped with pots and pans, a little fridge, a stove to cook on and a bed to dream on; and the manager trusted me to pay him in two weeks.

I got a low-paying job in the EOF (Economic Opportunity Fund) office at what is now ACCC (Atlantic Cape Community College), counseling students worse off financially than I was. Somehow, I made a loaf of Wonder Bread, an off-brand jar of crunchy peanut butter and a bag of sweet Red Delicious apples last two weeks. I have to admit, however, that the sugar packets and tea bags from the greasy room of the college officially known as the cafeteria supplemented them. No matter what Johnny Cash sang, nobody walks a straight line in this life. While I had time on my hands waiting for my first paycheck, I also had fleeting and not-so-fleeting thoughts about collecting the check and hopping on the next bus back to New York, where everything would magically work out. Luckily, in my saner moments, I realized returning to the city would mean returning to Art, and that would mean yet another act of self-destruction. So on my payday, I opened a checking account at Guarantee Bank, paid the back rent and a week in advance and bought some Gaines-Burgers for Freckles and veggies and beef cubes for me. I was broke but not depressed. I was going to go home and make a big pot of beef stew and walk the boards after supper.

This spiritual thing called grace was really working, but just to be on the safe side, I thought I should go to church in the huge, stately, old red-brick building at Pacific and Pennsylvania. Over four decades later, I live a short block away and still go there for concerts and to donate to Sister Jean's Kitchen, which serves breakfast and a hot lunch to anyone who walks in. John Denver, the singer, said, "Love is feeding everybody." He must have been thinking about Sister Jean's and feeling the grace flowing from that kitchen.

By the time I got a couple more paychecks, I was eating my way through Atlantic City with friends. I discovered pepper-and-egg subs from White House with Ron and pepperoni pizza at Tony's Baltimore Grill with Judy from Brooklyn. I found McGee's on my own because it was near the post

Visitors pose in front of Tony's Baltimore Grille on Atlantic Avenue. In the summer, lines formed around the block at dinnertime. *Photo: Sandy Stoltzman.*

office. No place had better fried butterfly shrimp, stuffed baked potatoes and cheesecake than McGee's. And who could forget having the daily sandwich special upstairs next to the Downstairs Card Shop at Gordon's Alley and then buying one of Hattie's homemade beef or chicken potpies on the way out. I read somewhere that Brother Thomas of the Nada Hermitage said food is God's love made edible. I have one regret. Mama Rita, I wish I'd been around when you were cooking at the 500 Club. You were a lady of so much talent and grace. Bless your beautiful soul.

All the good food prepared with love wasn't in restaurants. I can still taste the homemade meals friends made for me:

- Sidney's vegetable soup: The secret ingredient is a chopped sweet potato.
- Ron's grandfather's no-lumps onion gravy: I don't know the secret to this.
- Patsy's beef stew: There's no secret. But while you're putting in the carrots and potatoes, add a little corn and some green beans.

Later on, one unnamed foodie not only made me dinner but also offered me a job with meals included. He was working as a bellman or doorman when Resorts opened the first casino hotel in the stately old Haddon Hall. Free-spending male patrons wanting escorts for dining, dancing, gambling and whatever regularly consulted him. No waiting for a paycheck. No paperwork. No boring staff meetings....Looking back, I wonder if I turned it down due to no retirement plan. I was big on early retirement.

Thank you, Atlantic City, for surrounding me with grace for forty-two years, when I've deserved it and when I haven't. That's amazing!

Chapter 22

BEACH DAYS

Robbi Nestor

ummers in Philadelphia during my childhood burn in my memory, hot and sultry. Green leaves, so lately unfolded, wilted on the branches. Humidity dragged the clouds down like shirts left too long on the line. Rain would sometimes fall; it wasn't much of a relief, yet it provided drama to otherwise hot and monotonous days. Dark clouds would gather like a gang up to nothing good, scowling down on the ground below. The air would become unbearably heavy, like a sodden towel, and the big, slow, heavy drops would start, building up momentum until they hammered down thrillingly.

Six years old, I ran up the driveway in my bathing suit, arms wide open and face to the sky, just to feel that blessed wetness for a moment and to see jagged fingers of lightning probe the darkened sky. I wished that the electricity would go out, just so I could sit with a flashlight and read in the darkened living room, eating ice cream with a wooden spoon so it wouldn't melt. In an hour or less, the storm would be over and the heat back, even more oppressive than before.

In this kind of weather, the only relief a person could hope for was to head for *the shore*, usually Atlantic City in our case, about an hour or so drive from Philadelphia.

The ride seemed to go on forever. While the rest of the cars, low and sleek, with wings extending half the width of the car, blew by us, tinted windows closed to the heat and humidity, our two-tone snub-nosed Chevy sat high on the road. Since we had no air-conditioning, we rolled the windows down as far as they would go so the breeze, pitiful though it was, could blow through the car. Even my mother, who was always cold, would not complain. Instead, she closed her eyes to let the cool air circulate over her eyelids, as her hair swept off her forehead in lacquered arcs.

I knew we were almost there when gulls flew overhead and the land flattened out, as though some giant hand had smoothed it. The shrubs growing by the side of road grew short and windblown, and billboards for motels, restaurants and Coppertone suntan lotion sprouted on the highway like weeds.

Places to stay at the beach were plentiful, but instead of the giant hotels imperiously fronting the boardwalk or the low-riding motels, with their garish signs exclaiming "Vacancy! Saltwater pool! Color TV!" my thrifty father opted for old boardinghouses with worn cane rockers on the front porch. Though we generally had a kitchenette, we would sometimes have to share a bathroom, and the suite, though it was certainly clean, if a bit threadbare, smelled slightly musty.

These places, which would in a dozen years be torn down to make way for the casinos and lavish hotels to come, were bad news for me because they required some blocks' walk to the boardwalk, and I was impatient to see the ocean and to feel the wet sand between my toes. But the good thing about this is that if we were far enough away from the beach, we might be able to take a jitney, a small bus, bearing the names of places straight off a Monopoly board—Park Place, Boardwalk, Oriental Avenue.

The boardwalk assaulted the nostrils well before it met the eye. A thousand odors, many of them pleasant, like the sweetness of cotton candy, the tantalizing lure of roasting peanuts and the smoke from charbroiling hotdogs, mingled with the suspect hint of cigar smoke, half-empty beer cans and sewage. Hundreds of people traveled the boards by foot and by the small, half-moon-shaped wicker conveyances, topped by fringed sunshades, that I have seen no other place since, a relic of the good old days of my grandmother, when Atlantic City was the exclusive haunt of rich Philadelphians who might otherwise be found promenading in their straw boaters, white linen suits and long stiff skirts, parasols held high overhead.

All the while, hucksters of various kinds called out their wares. Atlantic City was the home of the original infomercial. The Vitamix, an early blender, in the hands of the salesman demonstrating its healthful benefits, produced a wonderful drink composed of pineapples, oranges and carrots. However, once we took the blender home, the best we could do was to produce a noxious sludge the color of a bad bruise. Half the charm of these items was the amazing sleight of hand the salesmen would demonstrate, calling in the aid of shills in the crowd.

The shrine to all things Atlantic City was the amazing Steel Pier. It was a long walk down the boards, but it was worth it to watch the prancing white horse, with its intrepid rider tricked out in a spangled swimsuit, dive from a platform tottering high overhead into an inadequate and somewhat rickety swimming pool perched on the pier below. And the freak show both repelled and drew me, with its inevitable shrunken mermaids in a jar, two-headed calves and the obese bearded ladies, looking dreadfully bored, with their multiple chins like untended suburban lawns, sprouting an occasional spiky tuft, consuming frozen custard cones in the shade.

But I still hadn't dipped my toes into the ocean. Truthfully, the beach at Atlantic City is no great shakes. I have since seen many other far more beautiful shorelines in Massachusetts, Florida, California, Oregon and Baja California, but for me as a child, with nothing to compare it to, this beach was heaven. The wide blue sky, full of looping skywriters trailing bright advertising banners, stretched out above me as I lay baking on the scratchy brown sand, where one might, with a little effort, unearth coins, rings and other untold treasures and trash (including used hypodermic needles and condoms).

The sea met this blue field of sky at a line I imagined as accessible to the surf skimmers and riders who, unlike me, the nonswimmer, strode and bobbed purposefully into the waves toward the farthest buoys. My father, hairy and smiling in his baggy blue bathing trunks, was one of these, and he wanted me to enjoy this pleasure as well, touting salt water as the best remedy for the eternal poison ivy from which we both suffered every summer, so he would scoop me up and throw me into the biggest waves, while my mother, another nonswimmer, wept and begged him to stop it before I drowned. I screamed, half laughing, half panicking, swallowing water, as the glassy green tunnels closed over my head.

Sometimes, escaping from my father's eager grasp, I would slip down the strand, in search of an ice cream cone or some other children to play with, trying to keep my parents' blanket and umbrella within sight. I would line it up with a landmark on the boardwalk, like a particular hotel or restaurant, occasionally glancing back, like Hansel and Gretel leaving their trail of crumbs—but just as with those two unfortunate denizens of the fairytale, when I wanted to head back home, the landmarks would seem to have slipped entirely from my sight. I would wander in circles, weeping and

Generations of families came to Atlantic City to enjoy sunny days on the beach. *Janet Robinson Bodoff.*

calling, trying to spot my parents' umbrella and towels among the thousands exactly like them.

By the time I finally found my parents, the salt water would have dried on my skin, leaving it tight and crawly. Sand flies would have bit my tempting calves and feet. It was time to change for supper.

This was perhaps the most embarrassing and unpleasant part of the day. Though I was only a small child, I was not happy about the prospect of stripping out of my bathing suit behind a towel as my mother pulled the damp, salty mess from my body, wiped me down with cold water and a washcloth and dried me with another clean towel. The scratchy dried-on grains of sand covering every inch of my body would scrape my legs and back like some form of exotic torture, as the children the next blanket over would smirk at me smugly. Though I squirmed and whined, my mother remained undeterred, and soon I was clean and dry again, ready to go eat dinner on the boardwalk.

Going out to eat for our family was a very momentous and rare event. My parents seldom splurged on restaurants, believing that home food was best, as well as cheapest. We always traveled with the same safe and boring roast beef sandwiches and watery salad mom made for us at home. So when my parents deigned to go to a seafood restaurant—since after all, we *were* at the beach, where the fish was bound to be fresh—it was something special. Though I was small and extremely skinny, I had a very large appetite, especially after a day of playing on the beach.

Once, the forbidden—and because of that, attractive—shrimp and scallop plate, breaded and fried and piled atop a greasy sheaf of French fries, looked good to me, so I begged and begged my parents to order it. Although they could hardly claim to keep kosher at home or anywhere else, they still felt queasy about me ordering such flagrant *treif*. But they relented and even nibbled a bit themselves, admitting that the shellfish tasted rather nice, but stuck to good old cod or flounder for themselves, no different than mom would have fixed at home.

For me, vacations have always been about doing something out of the ordinary, seeing new sights and people, eating new foods. But for my parents, who had traveled the world before I was born, this novelty apparently held little charm. The idea for them was to make their temporary digs as much like the home they had left as they could. For this reason, they packed enormous amounts of things—beach bags, towels, clothes, pots and pans, food and other goods they found to be necessary. There was always so much of this stuff in the car that I could barely be packed myself into a tiny square of seat, unable to move my legs. Though I always wanted to bring a friend with us on vacation, it would have been impossible to fit anyone else into that car.

We spent evenings on the boardwalk, where the saltwater taffy looped in unending pastel parabolas and snacks on a stick beckoned from every storefront. Since I was already full, what spoke to me most were the gigantic stuffed animals on offer at the games of chance where, for a quarter, one

Lifeguards keep careful watch over bathers at Albany Avenue Beach. *Photo: Bernard Jenkins.*

could attempt to toss a half-dozen ping-pong balls into a far-off bucket in an effort to win a prize. For the most part, my father forbade such gambling, admonishing me each time with tales of my notorious great-grandfather, who, he claimed, had lost the family farm playing poker, leaving his family homeless.

To reinforce the lesson, we would always stop at the toy store on the boardwalk, its show windows full of stuffed animals of every description, a cadre of creatures arranged around a synthetic waterhole: a nearly life-size stegosaurus, an antelope and two exceedingly realistic lions, resting by a stuffed palm. Magnanimously, he would allow me to pick out a stuffed animal (though not a tremendously large one—where, after all, would we put it?), and this generally silenced my pleas. It is worth noting that years later, my father bought a lottery ticket every day, breaking his own rules— nothing if not inconsistent.

Finally, we tired of eating, walking, looking, our senses frayed. Beneath a featureless silver moon, the ocean, as full of phosphorescent sparks as the night sky, thundered and thudded. We'd sit on a bench, silent, sated, satisfied with our day at the beach, a brief escape from the city's heat.

Chapter 23

ATLANTIC CITY

Elinor Mattern

In the just-past-dusk sky
the moon's perched on the edge

of the bay, money-round.
The moon becomes a ripply column,

a candle, a staircase to climb
across the city, a gambol on water,

a heartache, a misleading
brilliant bridge of light.

Moon on the bay. *Photo: Janet Robinson Bodoff.*

Chapter 24

SKINNY D'AMATO'S CLOCK

Molly Golubcow

As a kid growing up in Atlantic City, New Jersey, Skinny D'Amato was a legend—both famous and infamous. He was known as a generous and caring man as well as a confirmed gambler and party guy. From the 1930s until it burned to the ground in the 1970s, Skinny was the owner and operator of Atlantic City's most frequented nightclub, the 500 Club. He hosted drinking and dancing in the main room and alleged illegal gambling in private rooms. Anyone who was anyone jumped at the chance for a night out at the 500. Skinny enthusiastically mingled with his customers and palled around with local politicians, mob characters and stars like Sinatra, Dean Martin and Sammy Davis Jr., who also entertained at the club throughout the years.

When signs advertising the estate sale for Skinny D'Amato started popping up all around the neighborhood, I knew that this was my ticket to see the inside of his Ventnor home. Everything from memorabilia, clothing and furniture would be displayed for the public to see and touch and buy: dishes and pots from kitchen cabinets, family pictures—some still on the wall— bar accessories from swizzle sticks to half-empty Chivas Regal bottles and assorted tchotchkes on book shelves.

Now, don't get me wrong; as an estate sale addict, I wanted to see the goods. I always liked poking around in a stranger's house, opening drawers and closets and sifting through thirty, forty, fifty years of accumulations. There isn't another occasion where one can enter a stranger's house and

Crowds mob Dean Martin and Jerry Lewis on the boardwalk. *Courtesy of Kathy Dollard.*

go through their underwear drawers without accusations of being a pervert or, maybe worse, having the police called to come fetch you. An estate sale is open season, and everything can be fingered, squeezed and bargained down. But what intrigued me the most about this estate sale was getting in and seeing the basement where Skinny's son, Angelo, brutally murdered an unfortunate guest. Yes, I confess the posted estate sale signs fueled the fire of my morbid curiosity.

Left: Old Blue Eyes at the 500 Club. *Courtesy of Kathy Dollard.*

Right: Officer Larry Renze escorts Dean Martin backstage at the 500 Club. *Courtesy of Kathy Dollard.*

As soon as my friend Susan and I entered Skinny's house on the day of the estate sale, I charged down to the basement. When I got to the bottom of the stairs, I came face-to-face (so to speak) with a grandmother clock. It had a light oak veneer with gold trim, standing on a funky, four-legged pedestal. Although it was a nice-looking clock, it was not in working order, with its hands frozen at 7:40. But I was not in the basement to shop. I was there to get a look at the murder site, even though it was many years and many a cleaning ago. As I walked around the basement, I kept turning around to look at the clock. It was like that piece of furniture was watching me. I slowly walked back and touched it, realizing that this clock saw the murder.

My imagination went into overdrive as I pictured the clock's hands freezing at the exact moment of the murder. Suddenly, the perky woman who was running the estate sale started jabbering to me about how lovely the clock was and that it was a steal for seventy-five dollars. I told her that I was not interested, and she immediately dropped the price to fifty dollars. Again, I said that I was not interested and politely walked away to join Susan, who was sorting through a large box filled with pictures of Skinny D'Amato posing with guests, famous and not so famous, at the 500 Club. We found so many pictures and were looking at the 1950s hairdos and fashions when Ms. Perky Estate Sale Lady found me again. She just insisted that the clock was a great buy for me and lowered the price again, to forty dollars. I was getting a bit tired of this, and Susan abandoned me so she could get herself a souvenir shot glass. So I told the woman no thanks again and even pulled out a twenty-dollar bill out of my pocket to show her that this was all the money I had with me.

To my surprise, she smiled and said, "OK, twenty dollars it is—you drive a hard bargain. I'll write up your receipt."

As she dashed off, I started to panic. *How am I going to get this clock home? What am I going to do with it?* When I told Susan, she laughed out loud and kept insisting that that clock was meant for me. She asked a few healthy-looking men at the sale if they could help us carry the clock to my car. We had brute strength ready for carrying, but getting the clock into a two-door Subaru coupe complete with Heathcliff, my eighty-five-pound German shepherd, was a challenge. Like a Keystone Cops routine, we moved Heathcliff to the front of the car, backed the clock into the back seat and let the top part of the clock stick out of the open window. At this point, Susan and I were laughing so hard we were actually crying. The drive home was memorable: a dog, two humans and a grandmother clock that witnessed a murder.

Over the last twenty-plus years, the clock has been rigged a few times to keep time and actually has the most beautiful chimes when it works. A few years ago, a professional clock repairer came to the house and claimed to have fixed it. It kept time for about three and a half hours, and then it stopped again—at 7:40. I have always meant to look up when the murder took place in Skinny's basement but have not gotten around to it. My imagination likes to think that's what made the clock stop working. Maybe that clock was not meant to keep time. Maybe it was meant to keep secrets.

Chapter 25

MY SENIOR YEAR

Leesa Toscano

*T*graduated from Atlantic City High School in 1979. Memories of that year and of my best friends will stay with me forever. Atlantic City is and always will be my home.

My senior year was not all work. I remember so many fun nights at the Melody Lounge. It was on South Carolina Avenue and was huge in the '70s and '80s, especially if you were a teenager. It was a bar, restaurant and disco. Even though I was underage, my friends and cousins and I were able to walk right into the Disco. Atlantic City was always a bit loose where rules were involved. No one carded any of us, but we weren't there to drink. We were there to dance our asses off. The room was hot, the music was loud and crowd was there to party.

It was our favorite place to celebrate birthdays in style. Mine is January 22, and when I was seventeen, one of my friends brought a cake to the club. The band called me up on stage and sang "Happy Birthday," with the whole place joining in. Cake was passed around to everyone.

One night, punk rock music was blasting. Everyone, including my friends, jumped up and down instead of dancing; it was a wild time. Some kids were body slamming each other, and one unfortunate girl was knocked down. The band stopped and helped her to a booth. Management called for an ambulance, and she was taken out on a stretcher. She apparently was fine, because I saw her there on her feet a week later. Nothing stopped our dancing.

Top: The original Atlantic City High School. *Private collection; courtesy of Kathy Dollard.*

Bottom: Enter here to dance the night away at the Melody Lounge. *Courtesy of the Sutton family.*

"YMCA" by the Village People was a big hit in 1978. Whenever it played, everyone moved their arms to form *Y, M, C, A*. It was a song played constantly at Melody Lounge, sometimes more than once a night.

"The Great Josh's" Restaurant across the street from the old Atlantic City High School was another favorite hangout. Kids would skip classes if they didn't like what was served in the cafeteria. There were always lines of all ages waiting to be served. I remember the meatball subs were the best around. Students and teachers crossed the street to have lunch or dinner there, sometimes together. Kids with guitars often played there, and sometimes people gathered around for an impromptu sing-along.

We all loved the Albany Avenue Beach concert on Saturday afternoon. During the day, local bands played for masses of beachgoers. Everyone

Left: Weekly advertising highlighted the current headliner at the Melody Lounge. *Courtesy of the Sutton family.*

Right: Call the Great Josh for delivery. *Private collection.*

spread out their beach blankets in the sand, and families brought out thermoses and lunch boxes. They picnicked while listening to the bands. Lots of us danced in bathing suits at the foot of the stage. Some played volleyball, and others sat on chairs by the water's edge or swam in the ocean. People enjoyed alcoholic concoctions, and there was always the smell of pot in the air. Police officers were present on the beach, but nothing bad ever happened, and I never saw anyone arrested. My three high school gal pals attended every beach concert. The four bathing beauties, Debbie, Harriet, Jodie and I, were always up dancing by the stage in our bathing suits. We danced, talked to guys and socialized with the bands. We bought "fudgie wudgies" from the ice cream man, and we ate the ice cream quickly, before it melted all over. If it did, we ran into the ocean to clean our sticky hands.

To this day, I remember meeting an older couple walking their three greyhounds near the ocean edge. I went over to the couple, who wore "I love Atlantic City" T-shirts, and asked if I could pet the dogs. "Hi, doggies. You are so cute," I said, petting the dogs, and the dogs seemed to like the attention. I asked, "What are the dogs' names?" The woman, who had long, grey hair, smiled and pointed: "These are Elton John, McCartney and Jagger." The elderly, mustached man chimed in, "The dogs love music, too."

The aromas of my youth—the salty ocean breezes, the nearby hot dog stands and pizza—come back to me often. I remember the strong scent of coffee from Ireland Coffee, over the Albany Avenue bridge in Chelsea Heights.

Chicago Pizza in the President Hotel on Albany Avenue and the boardwalk was a teen hangout. They served the best deep-dish pizza and were known for their humongous pitchers of beer. Groups of friends met at Chicago Pizza on Saturday nights, and we were often extremely boisterous. Waiters

The sun sets on Atlantic City. *Kristian Gonyea.*

frequently told us to get quieter or we would have to leave the establishment. We managed to get quieter, but there were always other tables full of teens that were louder than us.

My friends roared with laughter from jokes and making crazy toasts while clinking our glasses of beer with one another. One time, one of our friends, Rob, gulped his beer, then laughed and sneezed at the same time. His beer sprayed from his nose and made everyone roar with uncontrollable laughter.

We had school meetings and birthday parties at Chicago Pizza. My best girlfriends would meet there, and we'd talk about someone's latest breakup or some other massive teenage problem we had with our parents or our classes.

I often said, "Time for pizza therapy." That was our terminology for a girls' meeting to discuss issues of the day over a pizza. Of course, some of our problems weren't so easy to talk away. One memorable night, we talked.

"You will be OK without him," Harriet said. "You know he'll want to come back and date you again," Jodie said. "No way will I go out with him again," I said, rolling my eyes in disgust. "How Deep Is Your Love" by the Bee Gees was playing in the background. Jodie blurted out, "I'm pregnant." We just stared.

"Oh, shit. I mean oh...OK," I said and added, "How do you feel about being pregnant? Do you want to keep the baby?" Jodie answered, "I want to keep the baby. He asked me to marry him. I'm getting married!"

I thought, *That's a great tragedy averted.* I said, "Wow. That's great. You are graduating high school, having a baby and getting married. That's life changing!"

Then Jodie, Harriet, Debbie and I walked out onto the boardwalk. We stared out toward the ocean waves. The warmth of the breeze and the smell of the ocean always comforted me, but this time I felt a bit saddened.

"This year is a new beginning for all of us. It is bittersweet that we are leaving high school this month, but change is sometimes good," I said. We walked along the boards to James Salt Water Taffy store at New York Avenue. We bought fudge and saltwater taffy. We sat on the bench and shared our sweets. We stopped at Million Dollar Pier, played a few arcade games and went on a few rides. As we tried to cling to our childhood, we knew adulthood was fast approaching.

Now Jodie is married, and she has two sons. She lives in Maine with her family. Debbie is married and lives in the Philadelphia area. Harriet worked several great jobs and traveled to some exotic places. I attended college, and I have two degrees. I eventually married, then divorced after twenty years. I have a twenty-two-year-old daughter. I am still living in the Atlantic City area. And when I have a problem, I still seek comfort on the boardwalk, looking out at the ocean, feeling the warm breezes.

Chapter 26

CW SWEETS

Leesa Toscano

Sweet treats have always been a staple of the Atlantic City boardwalk. Like most people, I always enjoyed sweets, and I also enjoyed working in a sweets shop. I was barely seventeen years old when I was hired at CW Sweets in 1978. CW Sweets was located on the boardwalk entrance at Resorts. I worked full time while I attended Atlantic City High School.

I was hired two weeks before May 26, 1978, opening day at Resorts, the first legal casino-hotel in Atlantic City. I clearly remember the days when the store officially opened. Management trained staff how to make egg creams and floats. We were required to memorize names of drinks and ice cream sundaes, which were named after streets in Atlantic City. Management quizzed employees on names of sundaes and which ingredients went into each item.

During product testing, sometimes in a hurry, when we poured and stirred ingredients into the iced glasses, soda overflowed onto the table and spilled onto the floor.

The manager yelled, "No…No! We can't have such untidiness. You have to make drinks faster."

He then asked me, "Leesa, what's in an Atlantic Avenue milk shake?"

Not being totally sure, I answered as a question. "There is…chocolate ice cream, chocolate candy bar pieces and whipping cream in the shake?"

He smiled. "Yes. You got it. Answer with confidence."

There were four of us during our testing. Victor, Rob, Helen and I worked quickly making our sweet desserts.

I learned early on. The trick was to add exactly the right amount of cream to liquid, both at a cool temperature, and to add syrups as directed, not too much or too little. To me, it was like a chemistry project because everything was precise.

"You mean there are no eggs in an egg cream?" I asked.

The manager glared at me, rolled his eyes and answered, "No eggs. It's seltzer, with cold milk and chocolate syrup. That is an egg cream."

"Oh!" Rob blurted. Victor nodded his head. Everyone else nodded.

Phillip the manager continued, "Pour three ounces of milk in a glass, then dissolve the syrup into milk first, then add seltzer and stir with a spoon to form the foam."

The manager had shoulder-length, curly, blue-black hair, tied in a pigtail. He wore dark eyeliner around his eyes. He was about twenty-four, maybe twenty-five.

After the food testing, we ate the concoctions, and this was amazing to each of us, because we ate more ice cream in one day than most people did in a lifetime.

Coca-Cola with vanilla ice cream was the drink we called a Boardwalk, but it was a Coke float. Another float was a combination of Sprite, chocolate and coffee syrups, coffee ice cream, whipped cream and a cherry on top. This float was called a Gardner's Basin.

We learned how to make sundaes, crepes and ice cream sodas. We prepared the treats, waited on customers, dipped strawberries into chocolate on a conveyor belt, hosted and seated people at the tables. I also worked the register, and when working the closing shift, I cleaned and closed the store. The managers didn't mind if we listened to the radio while we cleaned. We blasted our favorite station through three speakers on maximum volume during closing procedures. Sometimes we cleaned the counters and refrigerators, and we danced and sang at the same time.

One night, Rob took my hand, and we danced a salsa dance in the middle of CW Sweets. Two employees, Waverly and Doug, began dancing together to the radio playing "Boogie Oggie Oggie," then, in front of us, they both pressed mustached lips against each other and kissed. I was surprised! I had never seen two men kiss that way.

They said, "We are in love."

I said, "Stop kidding. You're joking, right?"

Waverly, much taller than Doug, placed his arm around Doug's shoulder, and they hugged.

Waverly swooned, "Doug is my everything."

I just shrugged my shoulder and said, "Oh, okay. That's nice." We continued cleaning the store.

Later on, Rob said, "Remember, that's why they call this place CW... Sweets."

Not only was CW Sweets an introduction to ice cream, but it was also an introduction to gay men who had become some of my best friends.

Opening day consisted of long lines of customers waiting out the front door to around the corner of North Carolina Avenue up to the Boardwalk. Customers patronized the casino and hotel and walked to the boardwalk entrance to get their desserts. There were lines waiting to be served. We welcomed each customer with a "Hello, welcome to CW Sweets. How can I help you today?"

Mayor Lazarow and his wife ordered sundaes that opening day. A television crew and newspaper reporters interviewed our manager. They flashed cameras in our faces and around the store, clicking away as the employees worked in a frenzy to complete orders.

Between scooping ice cream and putting maraschino cherries atop sundaes for parents and their kids, we helped at the candy department, cleaned the tables, worked the register and did other varied jobs. We had a half-hour lunch in the eight- or nine-hour day. Too many smoke or bathroom breaks were frowned upon.

Starting opening day and every day following, there were lines of people at the ice cream store. It was busy all the time, and I worked nights most of the time.

The staff was able to eat ice cream on our breaks and when management introduced us to new sundaes; we sampled sorbets, ice cream, malted milks.

When I left work to head home by jitney, my hair, skin, pores and my stained uniform smelled of ice cream.

I began feeling disgusted by the smell and taste of ice cream. You know what people say about too much of a good thing. For a long time after that job, I didn't want anything to do with ice cream.

Chapter 27

I WORKED AT RESORTS:
ME AND STROLLING ENTERTAINERS

Leesa Toscano

hen I turned eighteen, I applied for work in the gift shops at Resorts International and was interviewed by a manager named Gia. She recognized me from my volunteering experience as a cleanup crew member after the Miss America parades. Gia was on the Miss America volunteer committee, and I worked under her supervision. Luckily, she remembered me.

"Leesa, I already know how great a worker you are," Gia said. She asked a few questions, which I answered, and I added, "Thank you," with a smile.

She said, "I like your enthusiasm. We need someone like you to greet the customers." She added, "When can you start?"

I was hired to work in the gift shop in 1979. The company I worked for was Host-Marriot Corporation. They had acquired three gift shops in Resorts, and more followed as other casino-hotels opened in the resort. I began my career in the retail industry, and for thirteen years, I worked as a salesperson and was promoted to supervisor, then to human resources trainer.

There was an excitement working at Resorts. Managers wanted the toys on in the store to attract people passing by the gift shop. Salespeople were supposed to play with the toys. There was a bright red-and-purple parrot that talked, and it mimicked what anyone said. There was a dog that barked and jumped backwards, and a doll that said "Momma." People stopped and bought the toys. Customers spent hundreds of dollars on souvenirs. I spent days ringing up sales. I learned about suggestive selling, and it seemed I had the knack to get customers to buy additional products. Some of my best phrases were, "Would you like batteries to go with the toy? There are matching shorts to go with the shirt. We have lighters to go with the

Left: Members of the Resorts International staff in 1985. *Wayne Stockton Brown.*

Right: Julio Iglesis introduces R.I.C.H. (Resorts International Casino Hotel) the Robot. *Wayne Stockton Brown.*

cigarettes. There is a necklace that goes with the bracelet. The ring and bracelet make a whole set."

I was meeting celebrities and tourists from all over the world. I sometimes felt like a celebrity myself. Customers asked for me by name when shopping at the store. The Rendevous Lounge was across the way from the main gift shop. Music played constantly, and the musicians frequented the gift shops, buying snacks, cigarettes and newspapers.

Sometimes, musicians brought me cans of soda and peanuts from the bar. There were strolling entertainers performing throughout the hotel. There was a mime named Jordi who wore clown makeup. A robot roamed the halls and talked to customers. Wayne Stockton-Brown developed the mascot R.I.C.H the Robot, and he was responsible for working the robot.

Sometimes the robot passed by the gift shop and I started a conversation with him. The robot answered with a humorous reply. Customers laughed. This became a daily occurrence: as the robot approached the gift shop, I started a conversation with him.

The entertainers in the hotel all seemed to have lunch at the same time. I was invited to lunch in the cafeteria with musicians and lobby entertainers. A bunch of us—Joy, Jordi, Wayne, Stephanie—often walked on the boardwalk together on our lunch break. Joy was a singer in the Resorts band. Wayne was the robot performer, Jordi the mime and Stephanie a costumed entertainer.

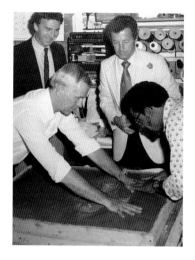

Johnny Carson leaves his handprints on a plaque that hangs in front of Resorts to this day. *Courtesy of Wayne Stockton Brown.*

One day, we decided to look through the huge Resorts trash receptacles and picked out playing cards and dice that had been thrown out. The cards and dice had a hole in the center so that they couldn't be used again in the casino.

There were T-shirts with the name of Resorts spelled incorrectly. Instead of Resorts, the shirts spelled out Ersorts. There were only ten shirts like that, and we split them up and took them home.

I said, "Someone made a mistake, and we benefit." The material was soft cotton, and I wore an Ersorts T-shirt as a nightgown for many years.

I auditioned for a part-time strolling entertainer job to work during special events. I was employed in the evening. During the summers, I worked in the gift shop by day, and I was a Resorts strolling entertainer by night. I wore different costumes at special events or greeted customers at the entrance. This part-time job was extra money for me; plus, I enjoyed dressing up in costumes. I was invited to high-roller parties, and if seats were not filled at the Superstar Theater, I and other employees were given comps. I saw lots of wonderful entertainment that way.

Dom DeLuise was in the gift shop almost every week. He wanted to be waited on before any other customer. I asked him to wait in line like anyone else. He wasn't happy about it, but he complied.

Dom said, "I have somewhere to be in ten minutes; I should be first." There was always someone who allowed him to go first in line because he was famous. This irked me, because celebrities are like you and me, but he did always sign autographs for anyone who asked, and so people always allowed Dom to be first in line.

Dom knew my name, and when he walked into the store, he yelled my name as "Leee…saw." He wanted chocolate potato chips, and we didn't sell them. I tried to order the snack, but our distributor did not have them. He was annoyed.

He said, "What kind of town doesn't have chocolate-covered potato chips? We have them in New York."

I said, "I'm sorry, Mr. DeLuise. I have chocolate pretzels." He rolled his eyes, shook his head no.

Dom wanted Jean Nate for men. I ordered Jean Nate. The cologne was at the store the next day. He opened the lid and sprayed himself all over, then he said, "I changed my mind." He walked out without a thank-you or goodbye.

Another time, he complained about the toys in the store. "The toys make too much noise. I can't hear the band across the way."

I said, "Sorry, Mr. DeLuise. We are supposed to keep the toys working in the store."

He answered, "I can't stand these toys on all the time."

I finally said, "Are you like this on set? I love your movies, but I am not sure if I want to see anymore of your movies because sometimes you are not nice."

He stared at me as if thinking. He didn't reply. He walked out of the store, then he came back in an hour.

He walked over to me, and he said, "You are a very nice young lady." He then bought a souvenir mug. I rang the sale.

I said, "Thank you."

He said, "You're welcome."

From that day on, Mr. DeLuise was nicer to all the gift shop employees, including me. He seemed to have more patience.

The years that passed working in the gift shops had given me the work experience and skills I needed for future employment.

Resorts had a casting call. They need extras for movies called *Wise Guys* and *The Pick-Up Artist*. The casting department was on the second floor of the hotel. I was an extra in *Wise Guys*, which was filmed in Resorts. I wanted to be an extra in *The Pick-Up Artist*, too. I missed the open call, but I found out where the casting office was located in the hotel. I knocked on the door. The casting director, a blonde, middle-aged woman, greeted me. I mentioned to the casting director that I was in the previous movie. She smiled and said, "I remember you from last year. You are Leesa?"

"Yes I am. You remember me from last year?" I had been an extra in *Wise Guys*, which was filmed in Resorts the year before. The casting director answered, "Yes. I remember you because you wore a hat, and the hat matched the skirt and blouse, and your name is unique."

I nodded my head. "Well…thank you."

I was assigned days on a movie set in *The Pick-Up Artist*. I discovered how much I enjoyed the extra work in movies. Extras are backup people who walk, sit or eat in the background scenes, and if you are lucky, you will have a small speaking role. Throughout the years, I appeared in various movies filmed in Atlantic City.

Chapter 28

PETER FRAMPTON AT RESORTS
IN THE 1980s

Leesa Toscano

$\mathcal{P}$eter Frampton walked into the gift shop where I worked. He was a handsome, smaller-than-expected man in tight jeans and a sweatshirt, about my height (five feet, four inches). When he appeared at Resorts, he stayed in the hotel. I was never a groupie, nor did I go gaga over any celebrity, but we would talk whenever he came into the gift shop during his visit. I commented on his music, telling him, "I enjoy your music" and adding, "You are very talented."

He smiled. "Thanks."

I thought Peter had nicer hair than me. His hair was long and almost curly, and I wished my hair looked like that. Of course, I never told him that.

Celebrities are like everyone else, though they may have more money. Peter was always with a beautiful woman with long, dark hair, who was taller than him. They were very nice customers and bought T-shirts and knickknacks with "Atlantic City" on the front.

We ended up talking about Westchester County, New York, of all places, which Peter said was one of his favorite places to visit.

Peter always asked, "How are you? You ought to visit London one day." He remembered my name, and probably the only reason he did was because, and he said this, "I remember your name because you spell your name differently: Leesa, *L-e-e-s-a*."

The lady that traveled with Peter was talkative as well. When she walked into the store, she asked about the beach and ocean and tons of other questions about Atlantic City. I never minded answering questions. It was

A jitney on its route. *Private collection.*

my home and where I worked and where I went to school, graduating from Atlantic City High School. The dark-haired woman never told me her name, nor did I ask, but she seemed good-natured.

She said, "I want to take that small bus. I can't remember the name of it."

I thought for a moment and asked, "Do you mean the jitney?"

She said, "Yes. How far does the jitney go?"

I replied, "It will take you to Gardners Basin, the Inlet section of Atlantic City and also take you the other direction to the last street, Jackson Avenue, Atlantic City, toward the next town, Ventnor City."

She asked, "Why is it called *jitney*?"

I told her, "*Jitney* is an English word for a nickel, which was the cost way back almost one hundred years ago when the jitneys began in Atlantic City."

Peter nodded his head. She then said, "I like the boardwalk and beach here."

I added, "Yes, I do too. I guess that is why I still live in AC."

Peter asked me, "Have you ever lived anywhere else?" I said, "Yes, Santa Monica, California, for a year."

The woman smiled. "I have friends that live in Santa Monica and Atlantic City." I nodded. "Cool. That's nice."

Peter then asked, "Would you like two tickets to see my show?" I said, "Sure. Wow. Thanks."

Peter and the woman gave me front-row tickets to his show for that night. I invited my mother. She was very ill and had just gotten out of the hospital and needed an evening outing.

From the stage, Peter looked at me in the front row of the crowded Super Star Theater and said over the microphone: "Hi, Leesa. Glad you could make the show."

I just waved my hand hello to Peter on stage. I mouthed the words, "Thank you." He nodded and said, "Welcome." He continued on with the show.

My mother seemed more excited than me and was acting like a teenager. She laughed with a giddy laugh and clapped as loud as she could.

My mother whispered, "I can't believe you know Peter Frampton!"

I shrugged my shoulders. "Mom, I meet a lot of celebrities at work." I'm glad my mother had a wonderful time that night, because this was her last concert. Severely ill with emphysema, she died later that year.

Chapter 29

SAMMY WISE

Bob Ingram

He hustled in AC before the casinos, and the chumps that came with them, made it easier. Everybody knew him: Sammy Wise. He always said his last name was no accident, whatever that meant. But that was the way he was. He never came at you straight on; his way was slips and starts and head fakes and bobbing and weaving. He was slight and bald and well dressed and always drove a new car, usually something with some heft, a Caddie or Crown Vic or even a Mercedes from time to time.

He knew people you'd never think he knew. One time, my friend George and I were hustling a screenplay about Big Daddy Lipscomb, the pro football player, and Sammy really liked the idea.

We were telling him about it at lunch at the White House Sub Shop, and after he picked up the check, he said he had to make a phone call. This was before cell phones.

He came back and asked us if we wanted to take a ride. We said "Where?" and he said, "Washington, D.C."

"I got somebody I want you to meet," was all he said. "About the movie."

On the way down, we finally got it out of him that we were going to meet the chief fundraiser for the Democratic Party, who had a houseguest who might help us sell the movie. Try as we would, he wouldn't tell us the houseguest's name.

We got to the guy's house—a big, white mansion on one of the lettered streets—around dinnertime, and the dude was already drunk on beer while he supervised the caterers for a big political dinner he was hosting in a couple hours. He actually had a small keg of Bud on a little cart he pulled around while he gave orders that nobody listened to.

We'd just walked in like we owned the place, and when he saw Sammy, he was so happy that he actually released the beer cart and ran over and began to kiss and slobber drunkenly all over Sammy.

"Sammy! Sammy! Sammy! You made it! The wisest man I know. Damn, if I didn't have this fucking dinner, we'd do the town."

He released Sammy and held out his hand to us. "I'm Martin Fairborn. I love Sammy! Do you love him, too?"

We assured him we did, and he retrieved the cart and asked if we wanted a beer. Sure. He had glasses stacked on the cart.

Then he sort of came to, "Sammy," he asked. "What are you doing here? Did I invite you to dinner?"

"No. No, Marty," Sammy said. "These guys are trying to sell a screenplay, and I thought about your houseguest."

"Yeah. Yeah. That makes sense. What's it about?"

"Big Daddy Lipscomb, the football player," I said.

"He was a very colorful guy," added George.

"Never heard of him," said Fairborn. "But that doesn't mean anything. I'm sure Hugh has."

"Is Hugh your houseguest?" I came right out and asked.

"Yeah. Hugh O'Brien. Didn't Sammy tell you?"

"Nope. He just teased us all the way down from AC."

"Typical," he said. "Hugh's taking a nap, but he should be down soon. Have another beer."

Now Hugh O'Brien was riding high then, with his Wyatt Earp television show, and we knocked back the beers pretty good to get over any stage fright before he showed up.

When he did, he listened to our garbled pitch and even wrote down an address where we could send him the screenplay. Nothing ever came of it, but that was a Sammy deal all the way: totally out of left field and into home on one bounce.

After we left Fairborn's digs, Sammy took us to a rib joint where we were the only white people. As soon as we hit the door, half the people got up and started yelling, "Sammy! Sammy's here! Hey, Sammy! Yeah, Sammy!"

It took Sammy about five minutes to get through all the hugs and handshakes, and then we had to go through the same thing after he introduced us as movie producers. Then we ate the best ribs I've ever tasted.

They're running at the Atlantic City Race Course. *Private collection.*

On the way back, I said to Sammy, "You know, a couple of those little kids in there were pretty light, and I'd swear they favored you, man."

"Yeah," he said. "I got kids all over—Black, white, even a half Chinese—but I love them all, and I take good care of them and their mommas."

Sammy had a very inventive mind. That was probably why he lived well, had enough money and had never held a job, as far as anybody knew.

Back when Atlantic City Race Course was going good, Sammy came up with a swimming pool for horses a few miles from the track, and a lot of trainers brought their animals there to swim away their aches and pains and get their running muscles in shape. Sammy said swimming was good for people, so why shouldn't it be good for horses, too? A lot of trainers agreed with him, and he made a lot of money. He even had to put in floodlights so the horses could go for a swim at night, after the days got booked solid.

Sammy was one of the gentlest people I ever knew, so one night in the old Haunted House, I became alarmed when he started to tell me about how he was walking on the boardwalk by himself late the other night, just catching the cool salt air, when three project kids came up to him with malice in mind.

"Jesus, Sammy! Are you all right? What did you do?"

"Well," he said. "I knew they were going to rob me and maybe beat me up, because it was real late and there was nobody around, so I started to play crazy."

"What do you mean?"

"I mean I started to babble and laugh to myself and ask them if they were from the city and did they know where Convention Hall was and crazy stuff like that. I even did a goofy little dance and sang about Little Bo Peep."

"Jesus," I said.

"Well, they must have been superstitious about robbing crazy people or something, because they cursed me out for a crazy fool lunatic and went looking for other pickings. I went home fast after that."

When the casinos came in, Sammy had an informal arrangement with one to just circulate and keep his eyes open, and he did so good that he ended up head of security there.

We had a laugh about that.

Chapter 30

TRUMPED

Janet Robinson Bodoff

Here we are, floating through a surrealistic fantasy
No sense of time pulls us back to any responsibility

Lost in the glitter like a plastic snowman in a toy globe
When slightly shaken we believe we are among the stars

No clocks ticking off the minutes
Time will have no meaning until we return to our individual realities

Caught in the ever-tightening grip of possibility
Oh, the possibilities!
The roll of the bones, the rattle of the cages, the folly of the jokers

No windows here. Day is night and night is day
Combining to become timelessness

Mindlessly wandering through the fantasy of being
Lost in the BIG TIME!

Perhaps we all want to be Alice in Wonderland
And let the Queen of Hearts strip us down to our basest being

Feeling lost and frightened, yet holding onto the hunch
that we are a winner in here. Out there just another loser.

Free gifts, free meals, free drinks…the carrot that draws the donkey forward:
the enormously, costly carrot.

In the end we all walk out with
cuffs frayed, clothing worn
and soiled, pockets empty

Back out in the rising dawn, rolling home, blinded by the light
planning our next visit to wonderland

Certain that it will be the day that
The bells will ring, the whistles will blow and the people will cheer

When we hit that prize of prizes, win of wins, payday of paydays
That impossible, obscure, elusive, gigantic
JACKPOT!

Slot machines stand ready and waiting for players. *Bernard Jenkins.*

Chapter 31

NEW YORK AVENUE IN THE '70s

Janet Robinson Bodoff

*I*n the 1970s, in a city that is only forty-eight blocks long, any one of those blocks could be lost to most people—but not the beach block of New York Avenue in Atlantic City, New Jersey. The hundreds of thousands who partied there will never forget it. In the 1970s, it was the scene, and you went there to be seen.

When Atlantic City was "America's Playground," New York Avenue was the gay playground of the country. New York Avenue was a rare gay resort with well over forty gay-friendly hotels, clubs and businesses in the area. It attracted gay and lesbian vacationers and lots of straight partiers from all over the world. They flocked to the gayest place in America. It was the party street where the party rarely stopped.

"It was one of the few places where we could feel safe and comfortable," said David Levoie, a Massachusetts native who came there on vacation and stayed twelve years. "A place where people could be themselves."

Most of the clubs were dark, with an aura of freedom in the air. Often the air was tinged with the scent of liquor, sea air, cologne and sweat. The rhythm never stopped, and dancers moved with the unrestrained pulse of the place.

Dancing went on all night. Clubs drew both gay and straight patrons to the fun and the action. Many clubs were mixed, but some, like the Ramrod, were for men only and some, like Chez Paree, were for women only (later, Chez became mixed). The younger crowd had a wide variety of choices; more

CHEZ DISCO

NEW YORK AVENUE at BOARDWALK
ATLANTIC CITY, N.J.

V.I.P. RESERVATION CARD
This Card Entitles Bearer
To An Open Reservation
At the Chez Disco

Brian A. Smith
BEARER'S SIGNATURE

Poe Foti
AUTHORIZED SIGNATURE

Top: In front of the Rendezvous are *(from left)* Tanya Treetop, Mabel Redtop and Sandy Beach. *Courtesy of Robert (Sandy Beach) Hitchens.*

Bottom: VIP card to the Chez. *Courtesy of Brian Smith.*

mature men went to Louise's on Snake Alley. Louise had been a Ziegfeld Follies girl and insisted on proper dress and decorum in her club. Snake Alley was actually Westminster Avenue, a tiny street that ran parallel between New York and Kentucky Avenue. On it there were many gay businesses.

Along with a powerful sound system, clubs had drag shows that were entertaining, risqué and typically hysterical. The drag shows, more often than not, were parodies of popular Broadway shows and the nearby Ice Capades that played at Convention Hall for the summer. Of course, on New York Avenue, it was called "Iceless Capades."

Every club had a house female impersonator in it. They would also work as the show's emcee and often as a bartender when they were offstage. Lots of them had alter egos with creative and comic names like Tanya Treetop, Tinsel Garland, Ruby Red Lips, Molly Makeup and Sandy Beach. Many others just took on female names like Dee-Dee Lewis, Kelly Peters, Willow Hendricks, Busty O'Shea and Carla DiPaola.

Along with drag, there were theme nights to draw in customers. There was circus night, western night, space night and under the sea night. Patrons would dress in costumes appropriate to the night's motif. It was akin to Mardi Gras on any given night. There were contests all summer, too. The Chester had a Mr. Buns contest where the entrants would reveal their bare bottom through a draped area and the audience would choose a winner with raucous applause. There was a Miss M and M drag competition, Best Package and T-shirt challenges, all in the name of riotous and risqué fun.

The business owners varied, from those who were open only to make money to those who cared about their employees. Winters always meant hard times for those who didn't save some money from the previous summer. But some owners always took good care of the kids who worked

Right: Chester Hotel postcard. *Courtesy of Brian Smith.*

Opposite: The Saratoga proudly presents... *Courtesy of Debbi Penn.*

for them. "Norm and Betty Ceil, who owned Ceil's Saratoga, served one-dollar meals to us and fed free Thanksgiving dinner to all the kids who had no place to go," recalled David Levoie. "Billy Mott from Mama Mott's bought Christmas presents for all of us," remembered David, "and there were others who just used us."

Summers were wild and crazy fun every minute, but winters were tough on the workers: not much money to be made, and rent still needed to be paid. One of the bartenders working at the Ramrod remembered, "Funny story about the Ramrod. I was very young working there, and I got my paycheck of eighty-one dollars for the week. The Ramrod, which was above the Lark, had an end of the season auction. I was drinking and bid my entire paycheck for a mystery box. I won and opened the box and didn't know what was in it. I asked David Lavoie what they were, and he said, "Your winter rent." It was a gross of Rush poppers. We sold every bottle that night.

My rent was one hundred dollars for a three-bedroom on California Avenue that I shared with Lynn Caters backup dancers…Those were the days."

Booze, drugs and music were all fodder for a good time. Quaaludes, Tuinals and black beauties were everywhere. Whether you wanted a "downer" to chill or an "upper" to stay up all weekend, they were all easy to find. Ask almost anyone, and they would lead you to what you were seeking. Poppers (alkyl nitrite) were on every dance floor. If someone opened a vial for themselves to get a rush, it was most often just passed to whoever was near to them. Just inhale and fly.

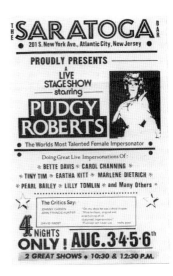

So many celebrities came to party. They would finish their gig in the best rooms in town and come to New York Avenue to relax. Seen often in the clubs were major movie stars like "Dorothy Lamour and Jane Russell, musicians like B.J. Thomas, Cher, Tina Turner, Peter Allen, Neil Sedaka, Davy Jones from the Monkees and Broadway songwriter John Kander of Kander and Ebb. There were comedians Waylon Flowers, Paul Lynde, Rip Taylor and Joan Rivers," related Bob "Sandy Beach" Hitchens. The stars came to unwind and be part of the party.

Many who spent most of their year living a pretty strait-laced life would come to New York Avenue on vacation to be themselves for a week or two. A history teacher from Trenton, New Jersey, would spend his entire two-week holiday in Atlantic City dressed as Barbra Streisand.

On any given day, you could see men in drag or next to nothing walking down the street. Of course, next to nothing was the fashionable attire on the gay beach in front of the Claridge Hotel a few blocks down beach. Sometimes next to nothing was even too much, like the time everyone decided to make the gay beach a nude beach. The police were called, and they hauled off a crowd of naked men. When their friends in the bars heard about the bust, they took up a collection to make their bail.

Many of the clubs had a cover to get in. If it got too crowded or sweaty and you wanted a breath of fresh salt air, you got your hand stamped for reentry. Dirty Edna's stamp read "PRIME BEEF."

"The club scene was a twenty-three-hour-a-day-affair," remembered Sandy Beach, bartender and drag performer at the Chester. "We closed for

Kornblau's Restaurant was a New York Avenue icon. *Private collection.*

an hour at 8:00 a.m. to clean up the place." That gave some of the partiers time to go down the street to Kornblau's or Lyle's Restaurants, where some of them were known to fall asleep falling right into their breakfast plate. If you were nearly broke, the White House on Pacific Avenue served up a decent-sized meal for less than a buck.

In recent years, New York Avenue and adjacent Tennessee Avenue have both become part of the Orange Loop, referencing the orange properties on the Monopoly board. There you can find clubs, bars and restaurants, but never again will you find the scene that existed on Atlantic City's New York Avenue in the '70s.

Chapter 32

MY LOST CITY

Barry Levy

I grew up in Atlantic City, New Jersey, a place whose very name prompts all sorts of reactions from those whom I tell. Few people are neutral in their opinion of the city; it's either the locale of fond family vacation memories or a place associated with decadence and gross excess. Sometimes, of course, it can be both. I was born the year a September hurricane devastated the city and region, a storm that remained a current topic for ten, even fifteen years afterward. I graduated the local public high school the same spring a sudden nor'easter rearranged the inlets, swept away beaches and destroyed many houses all along the coast, a storm I still talk about more than fifty years later. I left for college and military service and returned for no more than a few days at a time, most recently thirty years ago.

In 1980, soon after the advent of the casinos, a degenerate, tragicomic version of the city I knew appeared as a backdrop in a Louis Malle film, and I was reminded that Atlantic City had "floy-floy coming out of its ears in those days," as the Burt Lancaster character, Lou, tells it, clearly not knowing exactly what floy-floy was. But this is the Atlantic City I remember and that still lives in my memory—and my dreams.

Streetcars ran the length of Atlantic Avenue, more than nine miles from the Inlet to Longport, until the very middle of the 1950s (December 28, 1955). Hearing over and over again the motorman call out the stops allowed clever children to memorize the order of the avenues from the car barn at Captain Starn's seafood restaurant to the Douglass Avenue loop in Margate:

Vermont Avenue, Connecticut Avenue, St. Charles Place and so on around the Monopoly game board. As a boy, I roamed freely, without playdates or a ringtone tether; I even lived along some of the streets you may have hoped to land on when you were a child.

Union Station, serving the Pennsylvania-Reading Seashore Lines trains from Philadelphia and New York City, was at Arctic and Arkansas Avenues (locally pronounced *AR-tik* and *Arkan-SAS*, just as the town itself was spoken of as *Ah-LAN-ik Sitty*) In summer, the trains would arrive and depart the stub-end station on only a few minutes' headway, and large conventions, even in the off-season, brought many extra and extra-long trains to the shore. One could stand on the platforms to watch the excitement and hurry of the day-trippers, the tourists and the conventioneers and the rows of taxis and hotel limousines that lined up alongside the easternmost-arrival track 1 to collect them. It was possible to walk out to the roundhouse by the bay to watch the grimy, panting beasts being hustled on the turntable on their way to or from their trains. Until the late 1950s, many of the locomotives were ancient oil-burning steamers put into service to handle the heavy seasonal traffic.

The many upscale hotels that lined the most fashionable stretch of the boardwalk were open for anyone's inspection, hotels such as the Shelburne, the Dennis, the Marlborough-Blenheim, the Claridge, the Chalfonte-Haddon Hall and even the largest and swankiest in the tony row, the Traymore. A child could wander around their halls unchallenged, sit for a while in the lobbies, peer into the lavish dining rooms and the plush lounges or sit in the wood-paneled libraries and fiddle with stationery at a writing desk to imagine how the better-off conducted their lives. More daring local children used the pools and game rooms reserved for guests, not always escorted out when discovered.

The Segals in 1952 in front of Convention Hall. *Courtesy of Harriet Segal.*

In summer, for a single modest admission, Steel Pier, jutting over two thousand feet out over the ocean, offered two first-run movie theaters; live stage performances by stars of the day; a

132

One of the boardwalk's many arcades. *Photo: Bernard Jenkins.*

Bonnie Gordon and her son Albert strike a pose in a boardwalk souvenir photo. *Courtesy of Leesa Toscano.*

children's Stars of Tomorrow talent show; fun houses, rides and exhibits; and a long midway of novelties, food and games. Capping the entertainment several times a day was a water circus at the outermost reach of the pier that featured diving clowns and high-wire acts and concluded with a high-diving horse that carried a swimsuit-clad beauty on its reluctant forty-foot leap into a tank on the stage. On weekends, remnants of the big bands of an earlier time, like those of the Dorsey Brothers and Maynard Ferguson, played in the Marine Ballroom for late-night dancers as the moon rose over the sea, and a half mile away on shore, the lights of the boardwalk, the grand hotels and the whole city sparkled through the sea haze.

The sum of little things made for Atlantic City memories in summer: the droning, low-flying 1920s vintage biplanes that trailed advertising banners along the beach, their deep-throated radial engines straining to overcome a stiff headwind; a sudden shift to westerlies, bringing swarms of mosquitoes and greenhead flies into the city from the salt marshes, locally called *meadows*; the ten-passenger blue-and-white jitneys, some converted from bread- and milk-delivery trucks, scurrying along Pacific Avenue; and the Globe, possibly the last burlesque theater along the Jersey shore, that featured the likes of Cupcake Cassidy, Busty Russell and Virginia Ding Dong Bell.

And the variety of smells, too, most of them pleasant, further cemented memories: the cool, dank and musty air that came almost invitingly from under the boardwalk on a hot, still, summer late afternoon; the redolent breezes that emanated from the meadows at dead low tide. These were better complemented by the smells of early spring weekends on recently reopened amusement rides, their gears and chains freshly greased, their warming motors heating accumulated dust, the planks beneath them drying in the sun after a long winter under canvas cover; the scent of fresh peanuts from the Planters store; the line of frying doughnuts in Mammy's window and the ambrosial signature of cotton candy and caramel popcorn at the entrance to Steeplechase Pier. A couple of blocks down the 'walk, the spicy flavors of pork roll sandwiches wafted onto the boards from Taylor's, and farther still, the succulent meats and pungent cheeses hanging in the shops of the Italian Village on Million Dollar Pier would all leave their indelible, evocative olfactory traces.

For local children, winter often seemed to be the best time: winter, when most boardwalk shops were closed for the season and the 'walk, like all the city's streets, was virtually deserted by an early-hour nightfall. There was then time and opportunity to ride bicycles on the still and silent boardwalk, the usual rules about such things suspended or forgotten. And if it snowed, so much the better; to ride a bicycle or even walk at night on the boards through swirling snow was to experience an exquisite solitude, a sense of being the only child left to explore an abandoned city.

Nearing each year's end through the 1950s, accompanying the Christmas-themed displays and crèches erected on the beach in front of the big hotels, tall Christmas trees were set several blocks apart along the boardwalk between the Steel Pier at Virginia Avenue and the Million Dollar Pier at Arkansas Avenue. Each display and every tree was bedecked with strings of brightly colored lights and decorations. The most memorable along the row stood on the 'walk in front of Park Place, set like a jewel in front of the massive, rough-hewn stone and red-shingle Queen Anne confection that was the Marlborough House. Each city-sponsored tree stood behind a low, white picket fence that would not have stopped any would-be vandal, but they were seldom disturbed.

It could be said that Atlantic City's decline began during the noon hour, local time, on Tuesday, December 5, 1933. That was the time and the day that Utah—of all places!—became the thirty-sixth state to ratify the Twenty-First Amendment to the Constitution, which repealed the Eighteenth. The country's almost fourteen-year-long experiment with Prohibition had a dramatic effect on the seaside resort that billed itself as the World's Playground, but the slide would take more than forty years to bottom out.

New Jersey's largest shore town was the Las Vegas of its day. What happened there stayed there, and what happened there—the real money-making draws—included gambling, bootlegging and prostitution, activities that were, purportedly, technically speaking, well, illegal. Atlantic City didn't really have an exemption from Prohibition but worked out a nodding acquaintance with it at best, an uneasy arrangement at worst. In early December 1933, however, it permanently lost its status as a wide-open watering hole in somebody else's idea of a buttoned-down, bluenosed desert.

Founded as an island resort in 1854 by a railroad and some flinty-eyed, mainland-dwelling locals who used the buggy thickets and sandy swales for grazing land, the town never really deserved the Victorian gentility to which it laid claim by the end of the nineteenth century. But it was a pleasant enough myth, and well into the 1950s, one dressed up for an evening stroll or rolling chair ride on the boardwalk; adult sunbathers in swimsuits were chased from the 'walk during the day; perching on the 'walk's iron railing to watch the passing scene quickly brought a scolding policeman; and at nine thirty each evening, winter and summer, a citywide fire siren signaled a curfew for anyone under sixteen, a curfew more observed in the breach than the adherence.

Other things, too, marked the town's anachronisms and pretentiousness: just for starters, Atlantic City was effectively a segregated town. Although African Americans provided a disproportionate measure of the sweat and muscle needed to sustain its lifeblood service industries, they shared little in the profits. The large Black neighborhood, the Northside, was sharply defined, south and north, by Atlantic Avenue and the bay and, east and west, by the Inlet and the train station at Arkansas Avenue. The Black beach was at Missouri Avenue and was called Chicken Bone Beach by everyone; whites didn't go there, and Blacks didn't go anywhere else along the oceanfront.

And don't think Jews were welcome everywhere, either. Even though the city had a significant Jewish population, including prominent businesspeople and many professionals, there were well-known hotels that were assiduous in turning away would-be guests of the Hebrew persuasion. Italian Americans, too, were concentrated in a low-lying section back by the bay front that flooded often enough to be called Ducktown but whose bakeries and White House Sub Shop were—and remained—the city's delights. The moneyed families of whatever persuasion segregated themselves in the stately homes that lined the beach blocks of streets further down beach, where many properties had restrictive covenants to exclude minorities. African American professionals, the community's physicians and attorneys and teachers, were concentrated in nice homes along North Indiana Avenue.

But Atlantic City was a place for hucksters and hustlers of any heritage. Anyone with a gift for attracting a crowd and selling them kitchen gadgets, speedboat rides or trick-playing cards or for drawing in the boardwalk strollers to play panko or bingo or some other variations on illegal bingo, could earn enough between Memorial Day and Labor Day to live through the winter, return to college or move operations to Florida until May. One longtime boardwalk enterprise employed a silent mechanical man who strutted stiffly on the boards in front of the Haddon Hall arcade until he could lead a crowd of gapers into the gallery for the pitch by his confederates and the shills hawking lanolin-based hair products. The worst thing that could happen in season was a run of rainy weekends that would keep the shoobies, day-trippers with their lunches packed into shoeboxes, from coming down the shore on one-day-excursion train tickets. The harshest rebuke that Amos, an otherwise very gentle handicapped man in his forties who was a perennial employee of Steeplechase Pier, could hurl at an offending concessionaire was "Rain on you!"

But what would the child I was know—or care—about political machinations and official corruption, the business leaders over forty years who, in their ineptitude or shortsightedness, failed to reinvest profits to update facilities? Would I even, as an adolescent, have noticed that people increasingly traveled by private car rather than by train and could set their own schedules and destinations as a result, that they didn't need to come to the shore to escape summer heat in the cities because air-conditioning and swimming pools were everywhere by the early 1960s, that for the same expense—or less—people could fly off to the Bahamas or California or that what passed for entertainment in Atlantic City was simply and increasingly passé?

The 1964 Democratic convention was a public relations disaster for Atlantic City; the commentators opined and the television cameras confirmed that the town was a seedy, degenerate seaside slum, and it only got worse as the '60s wore on. Crime rates soared; seniors were effectively prisoners in their homes; abandonment and arson fires followed, until much of the North Inlet neighborhood looked like a war zone. A poorly considered, underfunded urban renewal project yielded only Pauline's Prairie over a significant portion of the South Inlet, and now, fifty years later, there's been little construction on large tracts except for parking lots. Just before the Memorial Day weekend in 1972 came a devastating psychological blow to the city as the moribund and shuttered Traymore, once the city's pride and icon of local propriety, was imploded into a pile of rubble; the public schools were dismissed early so the kids could go and watch.

By the mid-1970s, too, the decades of deferred maintenance, exorbitant property taxes, ingrained graft and a visceral inclination to clip tourists made it clear Atlantic City was no longer the World's Playground, an empty boast in the first place. With broader social and economic changes afoot in the country, any onshore, highly seasonal resort without a hook was doomed. A series of high-profile public corruption convictions made a perfect storm for change, any change.

Las Vegas gaming interests—certainly not *gambling* interests; the word was never used—stepped up with an offer the city couldn't refuse: new investment money and a chance for some of the old moneyed interests to take a quick profit and flee. Nearly all the major hotels in Atlantic City had been built in the first two decades of the twentieth century; some dated to the last two decades of the nineteenth. They were stylish in their time, perhaps, but vacationers now expected better accommodations and modern conveniences, or they could as easily—and more cheaply—go elsewhere, by car or jet. The major amusement piers that anchored the boardwalk were built between 1898 and 1906, and they had been so battered by repeated storms and recurrent fires that they were only the faintest shadows of what they had once been. The first statewide ballot measure to allow casino gambling, in November 1974, was defeated; a second measure, just two years later, sponsored by a new slate of area politicians and promoted in a slicker campaign, was successful. The first casino, Resorts International, fleshed out on the skeleton of Haddon Hall, opened on Memorial Day weekend in 1978; too many other casinos followed over the years, some only to succumb to economic downturns and changing tastes.

And yet, eighty years after the hour that commenced its decline, almost a century since its heyday, Atlantic City is still beset with day-trippers. They come on charter buses from cities between Baltimore and New York City and are picked up at street corners in smaller burgs no better off or more promising than their seaside destination. They don't pack their lunches in shoeboxes anymore, because they've been promised discounted buffet meals and plied with coupons to reimburse them even the nominal fare they paid to board the bus. They've been seduced into cashing their unemployment or Social Security checks in hopes that somehow—however improbably— they'll get lucky. To them, as that Steeplechase Pier employee Amos used to say to those who had a kind word for him, "Sunshine on you!"

But of the days before casinos, we old-timers can say, like the Burt Lancaster character in that movie called *Atlantic City*, "Atlantic City was something then. It had floy-floy! You should have seen the Atlantic Ocean in those days!"

Chapter 33

WE CAN GET THERE IN AN HOUR

Jessy Randall

*T*n 1990, I was twenty years old and just vaulting over the pommel horse of saying "I love you" to my boyfriend. We were in college in New York City.

Ross's dad's friend Danny invited us out to dinner at an Italian restaurant in the Bronx. I'd heard a lot about Danny. He was ex-mafia, or maybe still mafia, or maybe he was only ever on the outskirts of the mafia. He was a big guy, maybe 250 pounds, and Ross was under the impression he'd broken an arm or two when someone hadn't paid a debt.

We met Danny and his wife, Jeannie, at the restaurant. After we'd stuffed ourselves with three or four courses, Danny said, "Lemme give you kids a ride home." His car was a tiny, beaten-up Jaguar. He sped, of course. It was about eleven o'cloclk at night and we were almost back to campus when Danny decided the night wasn't over and we should all drive to Atlantic City. I didn't think he was serious.

"We'll pick up Tony and go," he said. "Can't go to Atlantic City without Tony." He swerved the car around, then zipped up and down streets I didn't recognize, finally stopping outside a dark apartment building on an empty street. "Back in a sec," he said.

A long while later, he returned with Tony and a wad of cash. We had already been squished tight in the Jag. Now I sat on Ross's lap, and Jeannie got into the back seat with us so Tony could take the passenger seat.

Danny told us Atlantic City was normally a ninety-minute drive but that he would get us there in an hour. I had thought that weaving in and out of traffic at top speed in a sports car would inevitably result in a ticket. I was wrong. We got there in an hour.

As we drove, Tony told Danny—and all the rest of us—that he hated his life. He was depressed, nothing was going right, his job sucked, girls didn't like him. "I hate my life," he said, over and over. Danny finally said, "So go kill yourself!" Tony laughed and started up the complaints again.

When we got to the casino in Atlantic City, Danny bought sodas for me and Ross. We were too young to drink or gamble, and Danny didn't want to get in trouble with Ross's dad. Ross and I looked on as Danny, Tony and Jeannie lost about $800 at the craps table. At one point, Ross nudged me in the side and angled his head at an entourage of bodyguards. It turned out they were protecting Donald and Ivana Trump, who were checking in on the high-roller tables. Ivana was wearing a shiny dress and a fur thing. Everything was lit up. None of it seemed real. We weren't tired or bored or wishing we could go home, though that's hard to imagine now.

We got back to the dorm at about five o'clock in the morning. I had class in three hours.

A decade later, after some false starts and detours, Ross and I got married. Danny attended our wedding with his new wife. We don't know what happened to Jeannie or Tony, and we still don't know exactly what Danny does for a living.

Chapter 34

I WANT TO GO TO THE CASINO

Phyllis Rita Cinquino

Aunt Rae lived in Longport, New Jersey, for many years until her death at age ninety-three. I visited her often and loved going to the shore. After moving from Philadelphia to Mays Landing, I'd see Aunt Rae weekly, usually to take her food shopping and "out to lunch."

On occasion, I'd ask, "Where shall we go today?" I knew the answer would be something like "I want to go to the casino." I knew how much she enjoyed the place, which made it fun for me as well. Actually, she was quite lucky there, more than I ever was.

I remember, back in the heyday of Atlantic City casinos, bells ringing and coins clattering for each win. One day, as I was removing coins from the bin to cash them and save a bit for the next outing, I instructed Aunt Rae not to move from her seat. "I'll be returning soon, so stay here," I instructed. Not hearing a word I said, when I returned, she was gone. Before notifying the search squad, I tried to locate her myself. Happily, I did. "I told you not to move from that seat," I shouted. "Oh, Phyllis, you think I'm a baby," she said. No, I never thought of Aunt Rae as a baby—perhaps a precocious child, surely not a baby. She was a strong-willed woman who would truthfully speak her mind, always.

After a few hours at the "machine," she was ready to leave, thank goodness. She'd had enough "tinkling" for one day; no doubt she'd return soon to that very spot.

A row of casino slot machines. *Photo: Bernard Jenkins.*

As we proceeded to stroll the boardwalk for lunch, I remember that the day was so bright, the sunniest of days. The ocean seemed to be creating beautiful music with the beach. *All is well*, I thought. *Today was on a lovely day on the Atlantic City boardwalk with Aunt Rae.*

Chapter 35

LEAVING ATLANTIC CITY

Emari DiGiorgio

After Jorie Graham's "Prayer"

In the smog-stained bus terminal, I watch a half-dozen pigeons, peck
along the curb, each a greasy Buddha nodding, absorbed in prayer, feathers
irridescing with the sublime sheen of motor oil on asphalt (black opal
smear,
anti-gravity rainbow), a procession through some
invisible labyrinth, one that cannot be lit by infrared or sonar—
resistance, the least of paths—this wandering not aimless, the
503 AC Seasonal sweeps into lot, hiss-kissed air, there
the birds scatter and lift, Ooo-uh sound that seems to burst

The ticket sales window at the Atlantic
City bus terminal. *Photo: Leesa Toscano.*

from reeds (it has those notes), a call that draws all eyes,
the flock regrouping at the fence (a line) apropos
three homeless men ask for change—
this is *In God We Trust*. This is the jackpot. This is everyone gets
what they don't want. I am the same, waiting to board, half-shaded
by the overhang. Less and less as I move toward the door, through which
body after body disappears, the faint wail of sirens increasing bayside.
Here, ticket in hand, holding it like some good luck charm
or my last dollar, I look away from the birds, the men, and say this is
what I have earned, I don't owe anyone anything. And if I ask myself
now what I meant. Ask, if I was wrong. It was something I didn't do.

Chapter 36

REFLECTION (ATLANTIC CITY)

Nicole Warchol

The seagulls circle in the glow
of casino lights
like they're flying above the sun.
Everyone else on the boardwalk watches
the laser show, how the neon colors
transform Convention Hall.
I watch the birds,
how their bodies curve in the air
as if tethered to a roulette wheel.
Why isn't the crowd distracted by this spectacle?
I wish I could save them.

Seagulls fill the sky. *Photo: Leesa Toscano.*

Absecon Lighthouse. *Private collection.*

From the top of the Absecon
    Lighthouse,
where everything is made of brick and
    mortar and loss,
Mary Lou, the keeper, told me it was
    decommissioned in 1933.
I look across the graveyard inlet.
The waves don't crash onto the
    Brigantine shore.
Here they charge with purpose.
There is so much sky above the
    clouds.

However, it is the birds I am thinking
    about.
I wonder when they rest their wings.
I hope they change course.
I hope they stop chasing the light.

Chapter 37

VIOLENCE: PRINCE NASEEM V. WAYNE McCOLLOUGH (OCTOBER 31, 1998)

Richard K. Weems

An evening bred and seeded from violence. Steeped in violence.
The violence began some months before, when my friend Connolly escaped his family life to drop $7,000 and many an alcoholic beverage in Atlantic City. Connolly plays craps hard and fast: $300 on eight, $300 on six, $100 or so on the pass line…you get the idea. He's the *one more roll* type—one more roll, just one more roll, who knows what fortunes the next roll will bring.

Connolly does not have $7,000 to drop at the craps table. Violence to his assets. Violence to his marriage. Violence to his body—Connolly commands that the waitresses bring him three beers at a time to hold him over until they can bring another three.

Money dropped, money gained, money dropped again, Connolly heads back home to northern New Jersey with a heavy marker to pay. At the Garden State Parkway, he guesses wrong and turns south, toward Cape May, the opposite end of the state. Somewhere near Sea Isle, he discovers his folly. A quick nap, and back he goes.

Oh, the tug that must have been at him when those signs for the Atlantic City Expressway emerged, as did those lights foreboding fortune off to his right…

He was to come back, bringing friends.

Mankind enters first, walking akilter with the effect of a psychotic distracted by his voices. Aluminum fencing reinforced with crossbars encases the wrestling ring. This is not your usual professional wrestling ring cage: it has no open expanse at the top, and it leaves a good three- or four-foot moat of space around the ring. It is the Cell. The match is Hell in a Cell. It has come to pass once before. That match ended in blood, much blood, and this one only promises more. Mankind is a defamation wrestler: this man has cut himself often for his sport. He is missing part of an ear, left it on a sprig of ring rope for the enjoyment of the fans. His body is a little soft, a little less than sculpted. Frankly, it is broken up to all hell. If all we can say about professional wrestling is that it is fake, then this man has broken his body all for naught, for no one is getting the message.

Connolly scores us a comp suite, dinner and tickets to the Naseem-McCollough fight through the Wild, Wild West, an extension of Bally's Park Place. Connolly and I and our mutual friend CG take dinner in a pseudo-Mexican restaurant that looks more like a Hollywood set than any kind of venue for ethnic fare. One expects banditos with filthy, filthy sombreros to come clinking in, demanding *tah-KEE-la,* their shoe-polish-brown faces scrunched up in constipated glory.

Everything is on the house. We start with tequila and beer, then on to beer and tequila, then a beer with tequila coming later, then straight tequila. We stick with the Dos Equis (which the WASPy waitress in the polyester rebozo calls Dos Equus), but when it comes to the tequila, we work hard to check off every variation on the menu—gold to reposado—but I respond best to the blanco, a liquid clear as water that fries at first contact but then goes down like sugar water after a while (some say that tequila shots get progressively harder to do, but don't you fucking listen to them for a second).

Before each shot, we strike our glasses together and call each other scalawags and ne'er-do-wells, for we are the high rollers tonight who wine and dine on the house. We are the ones duped in with free room and board in hopes that we lose big when we drag our drunk asses to the tables, so who gives a high holy one if anyone else is a little bothered by our raucity? We dump into our receptacles lubrication of the most alcoholic sort. We order dead animals steeped in fattening sauces and moan our approval. Drinking tequila is not enough, for this joint laces everything else with it: the barbecue sauce, the coleslaw, the cheesecake. The cerveza comes in thick, glass mugs that land on the table with a satisfying thump. We are big, ferocious men who have the power tonight, who are in the spotlight, who have a free ticket.

We are men doing violence to our bodies and condoning the violence done to the dead animals before us. The staff waits on us happily and reminds us the tip is separate. We are happy, meat-eating men who are glad to gratuitize well the wench who keeps our plates and glasses full.

> *The Undertaker is one of those awesome wrestling specimens: just under seven feet tall, massive arms enshrouded in painful-looking sleeves of tattoos. Mankind waits for him atop the Cell, and the Undertaker obliges. Mankind, of course, takes advantage of his climbing opponent and strikes the Undertaker on the side of the head before he can pull himself all the way up. But this is the Hell in a Cell—no one wants an evening of fake strikes accompanied by foot stamps for effect. So the two men soon face each other atop the Cell, and soon it is the Undertaker with the advantage, and soon it is Mankind in a precarious position: at the edge of the Cell, arena floor looking him in the face.*
>
> *Then, a move that stuns the crowd entire, even the naysayers that must be out there: the Undertaker flings Mankind forward off the Cell, and Mankind falls twenty feet or so onto a broadcast table. No matting. No buffer beneath the wooden table. The thing gives, but with a crunch that sends shocks through your lumbar and flaps your organs with the blowback. A crew much like the kind that swarms around a stunt double at the tail end of a full-body burn descends upon Mankind. Mankind assures them he is fine, but while they load him onto an ambulance gurney, he confides to them that the table hurt like a mutherfucker.*

Connolly, CG and I get to the Convention Center during the last preliminary. An Irish fighter is going for the title tonight, and the Irish immigrant contingency of the entire tristate area must be here. The prelims battle themselves silly, but the Irish want to see Irish, so a brawl has already broken out and the beer stands have closed. Our seats are in a heavy crowd of Irish, who sing and bleat air horns and wave flags and boast rugby shirts.

"We're among the Irish, lad," Connolly tells me in his best brogue.

"Aye, lad," says CG, "the Irish. You got to be Irish too, me boy."

I smile and agree and take manly pats on the shoulder. My name is Seamus now, Seamus O'Weems, and I'm Irish, goddamn it. You tell me different, I'll kick your face in.

McCollough enters with not nearly as much presentation as Naseem will. Our seats give a great view down the aisle, and before the McCollough entourage starts their march toward the ring, the Irish's wife hands him their daughter. Daddy's going to get his brains beat in for money, honey. Daddy's going to get his nose broke in four places, and everyone is here to watch him put up a fight, though all the odds say that he is going to lose. McCollough kisses the lass and passes her back.

Naseem enters under Michael Jackson's "Thriller." Echoes of flesh-eating zombies, but pansy-ass dancing ones. The boy can bob and weave like a snake, but who the fuck is here for a boxing match? We Irish want to see someone's clock get cleaned by a good Irish lad. We Irish want blood. We Irish want to see somebody get a good tarring.

Yet the match continues. Before the paramedic crew can roll Mankind out of the arena, the wrestler struggles up from the gurney. His right arm dangles as he makes his way back to the Cell. The fight continues, but there seems no way to surmount the level of violence already attained with the twenty-foot drop. Not another drop from the top of the Cell and through it this time, to the ring; not a leg drop by Mankind onto a chair covering he Undertaker's face.

The Undertaker bleeds from an incision he makes in his forehead while he is supposedly groggy from the leg drop, but we all know this trick. Yeah, yeah, blood, yeah, yeah. We've seen the older wrestlers, their foreheads a coleslaw of scars from years of slicing themselves with the razor blades they hide in their wrist tape. Yes, we know the actual violence that happens every now and then: we know King Kong Brody got stabbed to death by his own tag team partner in the locker room before their match; we know Killer Kowalski kicked his opponent's cauliflower ear clear off his head, and the referee felt it quiver when he picked it up to put it in his pocket; we know the drug ODs (Brian Pillman) and the sudden deaths (Quickdraw Rick McGraw) and those who got so goddamn big their own bodies crushed them to death (O hail Andre, Andre the Giant!). Oh shit, do we know how Dr. D. David Shulz smacked around that 20/20 reporter and never appeared in the big leagues again? So what are you going to entertain us with now?

Mankind knows the game. He hasn't massacred his own flesh all these years for nothing. He's set himself on fire, thrown himself on a bed of nails for crowds in Japan, dropped backward onto a miniature charge of C4. No way we're getting through this match without a little more self-mutilation.

While the Undertaker lies stunned in the ring, Mankind rolls to the floor and produces a sack of thumbtacks from behind one of the ring posts. A bright, shiny shower of silver as he pours them out onto the ring. He lifts the Undertaker and beats him back toward them, but the Undertaker does not fall. So Mankind jumps onto the Undertaker's back to stun him with a nerve hold, his fingers jammed into the Undertaker's mouth. The Undertaker lifts Mankind onto his back. One step back, then two. Mankind is in the air just above the thumbtacks, riding piggyback.

Then the drop.

Mankind rolls around in the thumbtacks for effect—thumbtacks on his upper arms, in his legs, all up and down his back. There are even some stuck to the back of his head! This match is over! This match is over! The bloodthirsty are a bit shocked, the skeptics aghast that someone would go this far just for an act.

Naseem has danced and woven and hot-dogged for far too long. McCollough has taken the fight to him—this kid is here to bust heads. We Irish have danced jigs up and down the aisles between rounds. We Irish have hooted at every solid punch. We Irish are hitting each other in a common wish to bitch-slap that Prince Naseem and make him cry.

The fight goes all the way to the final bell, despite the experts' best predictions. We Irish *know* who's won, and nothing the "Let's get ready to rummmmmmmmbllllllllle" guy can say will lead us to believe otherwise.

Two Irish lads next to me, two fine boys who have taken the armrest covers off their father's recliner and wear them on their heads, turn to me just before the decision is read.

"We're going to riot," they tell me, "if our boy doesn't win. Are you going to riot with us, boy?"

Fakir Musafar, the modern primitive, the man anthropologist Charles Gatewood called an "Astronaut of Inner Spaces," had this to say about modern spectator sports (mind you, this as he inserted sticks into his chest to hang from until he spoke to the Great White Spirit or ripped the flesh from his chest): he found the violence in them too outward, too much performed only by a few and watched by the rest. "In our culture, it's all secondhand... they're trying to have a physical life vicariously." Fakir Musafar sees enlightenment in those who have the courage to inflict the suffering upon themselves to rise above the body.

If this is the case, then McCollough and Naseem (well, maybe not Naseem) are high priests of having their heads bust, and the budding rioters next to me merely seers of their light. Mankind must be His Holiness the Battling Lama, the bodhisattva of self-infliction, maybe even the White Spirit himself, the entity Fakir Musafar was going to torture himself in honor of, all for the chance for a moment's revelation.

Maybe Fakir Musafar has a point. But still: a riot? I turn to CG and Connolly and tell them, "Riot." I turn back to my Irish brethren with those ridiculous strips of fabric strapped to their heads.

"Yeah," I say. "I'll riot with you."

The Irish boys punch my shoulder in camaraderie. And as soon as their backs are turned, Connolly, CG and I make for the nearest exit. The decision is read, and as we push open the doors, we hear the chant of "Bullshit... bullshit...bullshit..." The promise of some real violence, with cops and billy clubs and contusions and busted capillaries, is staring us in the face, and we take the back door out. Mankind has a reduced ear to show off his years in the ring, and believe me, it is an ugly fucking sight. CG, Connolly and I exit safely onto the Atlantic City boardwalk, living our physical life vicariously.

But then again, there still awaits a night of other self-injurious behavior. The violence of drink, the violence of gambling...the violence inflicted on the throat with the sucking of a damn good cigar.

Chapter 38

SUMMER ARRIVES
AND SO DO THE SHOOBIES

Meryl Baer

EDITORS' NOTE: When the first railroad came to Absecon Island, it brought an influx of tourists. They had to be rowed into Atlantic City. But when it was expanded to bring visitors right into Atlantic City, they arrived in force. For those who could not afford a hotel stay, a day trip to the shore was a family treat. To save money, day-trippers brought their lunch to the beach in shoe boxes and forevermore became known as shoobies to the locals.

TOURIST SEASON BEGINS, AND the shoobies are here (yeah!)!

The shoobies are here (uh-oh)!

The shoobies are here (is it Labor Day yet?)!

For those from another part of the universe, shoobies are out-of-town tourists and frequent visitors dropping anchor temporarily in our corner of paradise—our shore beach town. They come in endless waves for three months to enjoy the sun, beach, food and each other and to generally carouse and have a good time. You probably have not seen the ads, but *what happens at the shore, stays at the shore…*

At least shoobies hope so.

Most shoobies hail from the Philly area, although more and more are migrating from the New York metro and Washington, D.C. areas.

Like cicadas, which also arrive on a regular cycle, shoobies are usually harmless but very noisy, congregate in crowds and engage in rowdy

Bathers crowd the beach. *Private collection.*

activities. Except they do not die after cavorting. Shoobies simply disappear once summer is over.

Shoobies come around a lot more often than cicadas, invading yearly. First major sightings are a few days before Memorial Day weekend. They slowly trickle in, eventually becoming a steady stream of late-model cars creating traffic backups at lights and parking lots. Suddenly, on-street parking is at a premium.

Do not get me wrong, we want the shoobies to come. Sort of… Most have more money—and quite a few have a lot more—than year-round residents. They spend money in stores and restaurants and pay for lots of services, providing needed employment for housecleaners, landscapers, plumbers, beauty salon personnel, ice cream shop attendants—and the list goes on…

We need them for economic reasons. Most of us like to get a paycheck and buy stuff. We all have to pay Uncle Sam, and everyone here (in New Jersey) has to pay Uncle Chris.

And now I must confess: we were once shoobies.

For years, we drove down on weekends to enjoy the sun, the beach, the boardwalk and the food, to relax and store up energy for the work week ahead.

Then one day, hub and I looked at each other and said, "We are not getting any younger. It is time for a change."

Still employed and unable to hop cross-country or overseas, we decided to try full-time living at the shore.

So here we are, enjoying life and lamenting the shoobie onslaught.

But that's OK. Summer is short, and before we know it, the long line of cars snaking across our island disappears across the bridge, not to be seen again until the following May.

We take back our island, relishing the sudden quiet, the empty beaches, the ease of getting a restaurant table, the end of morning jam-packed boardwalk walkers, runners and bikers, and we enjoy the convenience of finding on-street parking directly in front of stores and other businesses.

We take time to talk to those remaining as the pace of life slows and the sharp autumn air finds us on the beach enjoying the last days of sunny, mild, beautiful weather.

Winter eventually descends, and peace and quiet prevails. By April, local events begin again, including yard sales (must stock up on toys for the grandkids), Restaurant Week and off-season specials, festivals, charity walks and runs.

And suddenly, it is shoobie time again.

Welcome, summer! Welcome, shoobies!

Chapter 39

THE END OF SUMMER
IN ATLANTIC CITY

Pat Hanahoe-Dosch

Midnight shift on the boardwalk.
Around 3:00 a.m., cops
and other streetwalkers stop
in for coffee, maybe an omelet or doughnut.
Around dawn, shadows
rise from under the boardwalk,
slowly, smelling of sweat, brine,
piss or vomit. Sand flakes off their clothes and feet,
absorbs some of the grease on the floor
as we sweep it all out, later,
scouring the linoleum with the abrasive residue.
We can't keep enough doughnuts and apple pie
in stock, though we buy them, frozen,
from a grocery store nearby.
Sugar and sand, sugar and sand, sugar and sand,
crystals or grains, all laced
with the guarantee of a slow drowning,
the surf's lullaby ahead, saltwater
taffy and fudge, parking lots, crunch
of shells and bone, behind, below,
horseshoe crabs, sand fleas and the cackling
of gulls as they drop clams onto the boards

A quiet stroll on the boardwalk. *Photo: Leesa Toscano.*

to break the shells, then pick out the flesh,
squabbling and screeching.
Nearby, the empty, wooden lifeguard stands
sit, waiting for crowds and day to begin.
The boardwalk is a line
for casinos, lounge bars and buffets.
A few shops still sell
T-shirts, taffy and hermit crabs
around the edges.
Pizza, fries, candy, video games and stuffed animals
clump around Central Pier, and then
there are just a few more casinos and, finally,
the inlet,
dark gray waters laced with oil and bilge
where boats still haul fish, tourists and
crystal meth.
Anyone can dive
among the wrecks
along Shipwreck Alley, the coastline
famous for its storms and destruction.
The boards lie across the sand,
shadows huddled beneath,
steadfast before impending winds
building gray, jagged boulders of clouds and rain
as the season's nor'easters blow in,
hurricanes gather strength southward,
gamblers drift out from slots and roulette and poker
to admire the view, the surf, the sand, the horizon
changing colors and striations as it darkens,
lights bobbing through the roiling black.
Boats scour their way to one inlet or another,
and always, the smell of brine,
salt and sugar from somewhere.

Chapter 40

THE PEOPLE ON THE BUS

Meryl Baer

The children's song "The wheels on the bus go round and round, round and round, round and round; the wheels on the bus go round and round, all through the town" played continually in my mind as one bus after another rolled up to the city's main bus terminal. The sounds I actually heard encompassed a combination of the wind, muffled voices, an occasional loud shout or greeting, passing cars, honking horns and the grating noise of bus engines and brakes.

Riding the city bus is not part of my regular routine, but summoned for jury duty at the city courthouse, rather than maneuver through traffic and parking problems, I opted for public transportation.

My bus arrived on schedule, disgorged passengers and prepared to accept a new contingent. The line slowly shuffled forward and boarded. Everyone flashed bus passes or stuffed dollar bills and quarters into the coin box ("the money on the bus goes clink, clink, clink").

The bus was crowded, but a couple of empty seats in the back beckoned ("the driver on the bus says, 'Move on back'").

Men, women and children of all sizes, ages and ethnicities and dressed in a variety of attire created an eclectic display. Many wore uniforms indicating employment at a local hotel, restaurant or medical office.

A couple of teenagers wore trendy outfits, but excluding the uniform-attired, no one else could be considered fashionably clad. And why do people with too many pounds insist on wearing stretch clothes detailing every love handle and—worse—delineating their butt crack?

The bus started moving. Travelers not yet seated lurched forward. A woman picked up her large purse and shopping bag, vacating a seat, and an elderly woman smiled and sat down. Other folks grabbed overhead handles or metal bars, bracing themselves as the bus journeyed on.

Few passengers engaged in conversation. Most sat stoically, staring straight ahead, oblivious to those around them.

A girl of about four sat restlessly next to an older, plump Hispanic woman. The girl, constantly in motion although never standing up, appeared deep in conversation with her grandmother. The woman spoke Spanish ("the mommy on the bus says, 'Shush, shush, shush'"), and the girl responded in a singsong Spanglish.

Everyone studiously ignored the disheveled man sitting in the middle of the back seat in his pajamas, fidgeting but silent. He must have noticed people eying him, because he started talking in a low monotone. The hospital had discharged him, and he had no one to drive him home and no money for a taxi. The hospital provided money for the bus trip. Apparently, he got sick in the middle of the night a couple of days earlier and had no other clothes with him.

A too-loud voice in the back corner of the bus could not be ignored. Initially, it sounded like a drunken passenger ranting senselessly. Listening carefully, however, I heard the burly Black man regaling folks nearby about his busy week at the restaurant where he worked.

It was Restaurant Week, his place of employment was fully booked and he needed to get to work *now*. Unfortunately, the bus plodded along, pausing at every traffic light and bus stop. People departed, others boarded ("the people on the bus go up and down") and the man kept talking.

A nearby passenger knew the restaurant of which the man spoke and cheerfully mentioned the place's delicious burgers, salads and happy hour specials.

A rather obese woman piped up, "I don't eat meat."

The man said, "We have the freshest fish and seafood, right off the boat. Never fried."

"I don't eat fish, either," the woman stated.

"We have great pork chops and roast beef"—and before the man could continue, the woman piped up, "Don't eat pork or beef either."

"How about chicken?" the man inquired, a cook and proud of his work.

"How is it prepared?"

"Half chicken rolled in a coating, baked; you would love it," the man responded.

"How about desserts? Love desserts."

Ah, the reason for the extra pounds on this woman who ate no meat, pork or fish was now apparent. She was addicted to sugar.

The man smiled and said, "We are known for our desserts."

The woman familiar with the restaurant waxed poetic about the establishment's seasonal fresh fruit pies and gluten-free blueberry muffins.

Our plump friend was not satisfied, desiring sweeter concoctions.

The man continued his monologue, now telling everyone about his wonderful boss and how he was going to be late.

The bus finally reached the man's stop. He smiled at everyone, bid us adieu and quickly exited, bounding up the street—as fast as his big, overweight body would allow—to his destination.

The end of the island was far—not geographically speaking, but in physical appearance and population—from the disorderly, chaotic city a few miles away. In this affluent, seaside resort community, not many people—except individuals living in the city but working in the outskirts—boarded the 505 bus to anywhere. Two worlds geographically tied together yet, in every other way, continents apart.

The few passengers remaining lapsed into silence.

A New Jersey Transit bus. *Private collection.*

Less than five minutes later, the bus reached my stop, and I exited, my slice of city life over. I walked the last couple of blocks home in peaceful silence.

Meanwhile, the bus continued its run to the end of the island before turning around and returning to the busy, messy city, its wheels moving as they did every day of the year: "Round and round, all through the town."

Chapter 41

PRETEND BOYFRIEND

Laryssa Wirstiuk

As we sat on the edge of the queen-sized bed, one of two in our hotel room, I kneaded Pretend Boyfriend's back to ease his cough. I worried he might turn inside out, like my blouse on the floor.

Reflected in the mirror hanging on the wall were two people in their underwear. Hardly knowing him, I hardly recognized myself.

Before this moment, the closest I'd ever been to Pretend Boyfriend was holding my iced coffee—venti, black, two Splendas—and checking to see where his fingers had broken the condensation on the clear plastic cup. I would spend my mornings trying my best to align my own fingers to this pattern, even though his fingers were longer and thicker.

"Are you okay?" I asked. "Should I get you a glass of water?"

I should have gotten the water without asking, but I wanted him to give me permission to stay in bed.

"How about a glass of vodka?"

He reached for the bottle of Grey Goose on the nightstand and poured vodka into two plastic bathroom cups. I couldn't have poured it better myself.

Pretend Boyfriend and I had met at the Starbucks in downtown Hoboken, which I visited every morning on my way to work and again during my lunch break. Even though the second coffee would make my hands shake, I wanted an excuse to see him twice in one day.

An Atlantic City hotel room.
Photo: Leesa Toscano.

He began to recognize me every time I walked up to the cash register. Soon, I didn't even need to tell the cashier my order because Pretend Boyfriend would see me and ask, with a smile, "The usual?"

We crunched the hotel-supplied cups together. He stood up, wearing nothing but his boxer shorts and dress socks. I watched him go to the bathroom to brush his teeth and shave.

I hoped that I wouldn't have to answer the hotel door for any of his friends—they would be arriving soon. How would I know what to say? I didn't even know Pretend Boyfriend's real name.

Unlike the other baristas, Pretend Boyfriend never wore a nametag and told me to call him "Slice" when I asked him his name. He was tall enough that I could see him over the espresso machine, and he wore his Starbucks cap slightly elevated from his skull so that his dark, curly hair stuck out from the sides of the hat.

"I don't wear my nametag because I really don't like my real name, and my manager won't let me use my nickname."

My throat had started to hurt that morning, but I didn't want to complain to Pretend Boyfriend because he had been coughing for days. Sharing all those green plastic straws with him must have contaminated me. We had been spending time together in the afternoons, when I came in for my second coffee and he was removing his apron for his lunch break.

Usually, during his breaks, we would sit in two armchairs by the window overlooking Newark Street. During those conversations, I learned that Pretend Boyfriend had also grown up in New Jersey, only minutes away from where my parents lived. I discovered that he was working as a barista to pay his way through graduate school for physical therapy. He attended classes in the late afternoons and early evenings.

"What do you like best about New Jersey?" I asked.

The way he stared out the window made me wonder if the answer could be found on the street. His gaze fell on a young woman carrying a tote bag from Caesar's hotel and casino.

"I think I would like Atlantic City best, but I've never been there," he said. "I'm thinking about arranging a trip with my friends."

"I'd love to go to Atlantic City," I said. "Can I come too?"

I had only been wishfully joking, but he seemed to like the idea.

"Sure, as long as you don't mind my friends," said Pretend Boyfriend.

Pretend Boyfriend stuck his head out of the bathroom to show me his face lathered with shaving cream. He started waving his hands in the air and kicking his legs in an effort to make me laugh. We had consumed enough vodka for me to find this funny and for him to continue.

He was so handsome, I almost forgot that he wasn't mine. I felt so comfortable around him that I couldn't believe we had never even kissed.

A knock on the door interrupted my admiration.

"Oh, your friends must be here!"

"No, that's just room service," he said. "I ordered a bottle of champagne while you were fixing your makeup."

"Just a minute!" I shouted. I quickly stepped into my strapless black dress and zipped it up with one hand. What I called the "one-handed blind zip" was a technique I had learned out of necessity. I was always getting dressed alone.

I accepted the bottle of champagne and held it up for Pretend Boyfriend.

"Cristal?" I asked.

"We didn't come all the way to Atlantic City to drink cheap alcohol," he replied.

He popped the cork. The champagne spilling made a dark island on the blue carpet and dampened the dress socks that Pretend Boyfriend had pulled high over his hairy calves.

"Be careful," I said.

But I loved his carelessness. I envied his complete disregard for the hotel room floor as he urgently passed me the overfilled plastic cup of champagne. The golden liquid spilled onto his hand, which he offered me. I licked his knuckle and tried to read his reaction. He was focused on filling the plastic cups.

"When are your friends coming?"

"I'm not sure," he said. "They like to make their decisions at the last minute."

Another knock at the door interrupted us. The young woman standing in the hallway had clear, almost translucent skin. She was carrying a purse I liked so much that I wanted to hug her so I could touch the soft leather. Her black dress looked too much like mine.

I surprised myself by asking for a hug but was even more surprised by her response: her arms found their way around me, and her mouth planted a firm kiss on my forehead.

We shared our champagne and drank some of the whiskey that she offered as a gift. Ashley reminded me of another Starbucks regular who brought her plastic cup and asked for refills of iced coffee without the ice. Whenever the teenaged customer entered the store, Pretend Boyfriend would walk away from the counter and let another employee take her order.

The teenager always got her way, always had her cup filled with cold coffee, minus the ice. Then she would dump half of her coffee into the trash and refill the cup with milk from the silver canister on the serving tray.

Neither Pretend Boyfriend nor I understood the appeal of cold coffee without ice. In my opinion, coffee was only good hot enough or ice cold. After weeks of this, I started to wonder when Pretend Boyfriend would ask me on a proper date. One day, when the teenager came in for her iced coffee without ice, she inspired me to say something bold to Pretend Boyfriend.

"Iced coffee without ice. It's kind of like us, right? A relationship without the relationship," I said. "The elemental part is missing."

Pretend Boyfriend just laughed. I always assumed that he didn't want a relationship because he was so busy with school. Embarrassed by my own boldness, I turned my attention to the teenager.

"I hope this isn't weird, but I've noticed that you always order iced coffee without the ice. Why do you do that?"

"Because I get more coffee. The ice takes up a lot of space. It's a total rip-off," she said. "Try it sometime. The coffee may not be as cold, but you'll get more of it."

I applied her reasoning to my relationship with Pretend Boyfriend. I wondered if dating him would ruin our lunchtime conversations, which were the highlight of my weekdays.

After Ashley and I finished with our last coats of mascara and final sprays of perfume, the three of us left the hotel and hailed a cab to take us to the dance club.

"Should we wait for your other friends?" I asked.

"I'm still waiting to hear from them," he said. "I think we should just start our night instead of waiting."

Pretend Boyfriend and I sat in the back of the cab, and he grabbed my hand. Ashley made small talk with the balding head next to her.

The windows were wide open, and the lights on the street reminded me of fireflies, the way they looked when I used to do somersaults down the hill in my parents' backyard. My hair stuck to my lips, but I was so grateful for the warm night blowing on my face that I didn't even bother to pull the strands from the tacky gloss.

Pretend Boyfriend was twirling the large rhinestone ring on my finger, and I held on to the moment so tightly that I must have left marks.

"Why are you so happy?" asked the cab driver.

He had to shout because the breeze coming through the windows made him sound like he was underwater. Ashley was waving her arms in the air, and I leaned forward to pull up her strapless dress, which had fallen too low on her breasts.

When we arrived at the Borgata, we all stepped out of the cab. Ashley and I fumbled in our small purses for cash, but Pretend Boyfriend waved his hand and paid the driver.

He took one of us on each arm, and we walked the red carpet into the hotel. Where was the paparazzo jumping out from behind a potted plant? Where were the flashbulbs exploding? The club was filled nearly to capacity, and the music was thumping so loudly I was sure that my heartbeat readjusted itself to match the new beat. The girls dancing on the raised platforms were wearing shorts that hugged their curves like someone trying to hold on to a memory that has been lost. Men who had come without women were standing around the platforms dripping condensation from their drinks onto the front of their pants.

Pretend Boyfriend bought us vodka sodas, and we found a place to stand so we could assess the situation before entering it.

Ashley noticed an acquaintance across the bar and disappeared with him for at least a half hour while Pretend Boyfriend and I danced. When she found us again, her eyes were glazed.

Ashley's acquaintance found her and pulled her away by her upper arm. When Ashley returned a second time, her lipstick was smeared across her cheek, and her ankle was wobbling so much I had to hold her hips to steady her. She wouldn't make eye contact.

"He's not paying attention to me," she said. Her eyeliner had blended like thick charcoal pencil around her wet eyes. "Don't worry about it, Ashley. He's not worth it," said Pretend Boyfriend. "Have another drink."

"That's the last thing she needs," I whispered to Pretend Boyfriend.

I pulled Pretend Boyfriend onto the dance floor and made him dance closer to me. He was stealing glances at the girls dancing on the raised platforms, but what reason did I have to be jealous?

Ashley followed us and hung herself on Pretend Boyfriend's shoulder like a crumpled dress. She was sobbing.

"What's wrong, Ashley? Everything is okay. Be glad you have friends who care about you and who will make sure you'll get home safely."

That's when I realized that none of Pretend Boyfriend's other friends had arrived. But I had no use for more strangers—dealing with Ashley was overwhelming enough. I couldn't stand to see other young women cry over men.

I tried to frown at her, but I was so drunk that parts of my face had gone numb. Was Pretend Boyfriend still kissing me?

"Please don't cry," I said. "He's not worth it."

"I don't know how I'm going to get home," she said. "I have to work tomorrow."

"What? You told me you have the day off," said Pretend Boyfriend. "You're in no shape to drive home. You better spend the night with us. We have two beds, you know."

"First, I screw up my chances with that guy," said Ashley. "Now I'm going to ruin your night."

I wasn't sure what to say. How could she ruin my night with Pretend Boyfriend if I didn't know what kind of night we were supposed to have? I let Pretend Boyfriend respond. Did he think there was anything to ruin?

"You're not ruining anything. We're all friends here," he said. "And you need to be safe."

Part of me wished that Pretend Boyfriend would tell her to take a cab home, but letting Ashley stay with us was the right thing to do.

On our way out, Pretend Boyfriend was no longer the male celebrity with a girl on each arm. This time, Pretend Boyfriend and I had to hold Ashley, who was thrashing like a panicked bird.

She would not stop talking about how she had ruined our night, and her words made me glance at Pretend Boyfriend to observe his reaction. But he didn't seem to think twice about it. He just kept looking at me and shaking his head.

In the hotel room, Ashley remained awake long enough to watch Pretend Boyfriend perform for us. In an effort to distract Ashley from her sadness, Pretend Boyfriend stripped down to his boxers and button-down shirt and danced to music that I couldn't hear.

The dancing made him cough again. I was surprised we had both been able to suppress our coughing. My head hurt a little, but I couldn't tell if it was from the alcohol or because I was really sick. Pretend Boyfriend's coughing fit was a sign that the night had ended.

Ashley slept in one bed. Pretend Boyfriend and I slept together in the other bed, but he rolled far to one side. He kissed me on the cheek before turning away.

"I don't want you to get sick, Veda," he said.

But I was already sick.

In the morning, I heard Ashley leave, but I was still drunk and too tired to say goodbye. I heard Pretend Boyfriend get up to help her with her things and then fell asleep again.

When I woke a second time, I found Pretend Boyfriend in my bed in an empty room. I was wearing only my panties and a black camisole tank top.

Pretend Boyfriend was sleeping or pretending to sleep. I started to rub his leg with my foot, hoping he would move closer to me. He was still on the other side of the bed with his face turned away. Finally, he moved, and I touched his shoulder.

"Come closer, I'm cold," I said.

I was practically begging him to have his way with me. Shouldn't I have been the one refusing him? I thought about the night before and the way he couldn't keep his hands off me on the dance floor. Presented with an opportunity, why wasn't he taking advantage of it? He moved closer but didn't try to kiss me.

"I'm sick, Veda. It's better if I stay over here."

I moved his hand to where he could feel that I wasn't wearing any pants. He seemed more startled and scared than aroused or interested. I climbed on top of him, kissing his forehead and his cheeks, but he dodged my kisses and avoided my mouth.

"Don't you want me?" I asked. "We finally have each other to ourselves. We should take advantage of it."

"I don't feel well," said Pretend Boyfriend. "And I don't want to complicate what we have."

"But I want you, can't you see that?" I said.

"I don't want to be that jerk, you know, when I become too busy with school. I know you're a good girl, and I don't want to be the one responsible for making you sad," he said.

"Are you really going to turn me down? I'm ready to go."

"I don't have condoms, anyway," he said.

"I brought condoms," I said.

To some, having condoms might mean that I was well prepared. When I heard my own voice, I knew that I was revealing my high expectations. I started to cry but moved away from him, turning so that he couldn't see my face.

"Are you absolutely sure?" he asked.

I nodded, even though I knew the sex could not possibly be good or fulfilling, not after all this talk. But I had already asked for it.

He climbed on top of me and turned his face away to cough. He kissed my forehead and my cheek, but he wouldn't kiss me on the lips. He moved his hand over my crotch, then worked his fingers under my panties like a plumber trying to unclog a drain for an anxious customer.

I closed my eyes. I didn't want to see him avoiding them. When he finished, I was grateful and asked for nothing more. I knew we'd never have sex again.

Pretend Boyfriend started coughing, and my throat burned so badly I almost couldn't swallow. I put on a pair of jeans because I was shivering.

When we finally decided to get out of bed, the day seemed to start the way it should have started. We took turns showering, got dressed, gathered our things and went downstairs for breakfast. We ordered coffee and eggs, and the only time that either of us mentioned the sex was when Pretend Boyfriend asked me if I was using birth control.

I nodded. Then he nodded.

"So, what happened to your friends last night?" I asked.

"They can be flaky," he said. "But you got to meet Ashley. She would never miss a night in Atlantic City."

"Will she be okay?" I asked, though I wanted to replace the "she" with an "I."

"She just chases the wrong guys," he said.

After breakfast, we used the rest of the money that we had budgeted for our trip on slot machines and tables. Pretend Boyfriend had never played roulette, so I taught him what I knew, which wasn't very much. We sat close to one another, whispering comments and giggling about the other people at the table. Together, we won a few hundred dollars, and he let me use his chips when I ran out of my own.

"I love this game," said Pretend Boyfriend. "Thanks so much for teaching me how to play. I wouldn't have tried it by myself."

The dealer kept glaring at us because we were talking too loudly and forgetting to remove our hands from the table between bets. I could sense that she wanted us to leave. We placed the last of our chips on red, and it hit. But the dealer shoved our chips away with the other losers.

"Hey! We bet on red," I said.

"Nope. I already moved the chips. You lose."

"But she's right," said Pretend Boyfriend.

The dealer called for a security guard to review what the camera had recorded, and we were sure we would be able to retrieve our money. But the security guard returned from the camera, accused us of cheating and asked us to leave.

Angry and broke, Pretend Boyfriend and I both acknowledged that our trip was over. We checked out of the hotel and waited for the valet to retrieve our cars. I started to cough so uncontrollably that I could feel parts of my breakfast rising up my throat. To ease my burning sinuses, I pressed my fingers into my forehead.

Pretend Boyfriend hugged me. He pulled a small tin of cough drops from his pocket and offered me a cherry-flavored lozenge. The sweet, melting medicine soothed the dry scratch and relieved my pain.

"I was worried this would happen," he said.

Chapter 42

A SHORE TOWN'S SOLILOQUY

Shelley Andress Cohen

I am Atlantic City, once America's
  playground,
now a petrified mermaid, an aged
  crone
powdered with stale promises
Remember when money rolled in
  like foam
rising on the waves, when hucksters
  hawked me
to gapers green with cash
Remember your sunburned
  escapades,
in my cotton candyland, moonlit
revels where
sex mixed with sand
Gone are my moneydrenched
amusements,

bathing beauties, high diving horses
  jumping
fear struck
into drums of water
Crumbling casino towers now crust
my Boardwalk, brightlylit
barricades,
my latest onetrick
ponies

Still I am a shellstudded
goddess
swaying on a splintered pedestal,
reconfigured, reinvented, redux
I'm your Missed America cresting on
fortune's currents, a gift to gamblers
betting against the tide

Night falls on the boardwalk. *Photo: Shaun R. Smith.*

Chapter 43

WHEN YOUR FATHER'S
A GAMBLER,
YOU GO TO ATLANTIC CITY

Nicole Warchol

How docile he has become.
Settled on a stool, transfixed
by wheels that spin.
He presses buttons and yanks on levers,
believing Fortune favors the tame.

But I've learned only fools waste
their cash on felt green tables.

I slink out of the double doors,
refusing to become another captive.
I tread lightly down petrified planks,
sidestepping seagulls that swoop down
from smoky skies.
I hug the storefront windows
where shopkeepers lie in wait,
ready to lure the crowd inside.
"Buy a T-shirt, a keychain shaped like a flip-flop,
half a pound of coconut-flavored taffy."

Checking the racing results from the Atlantic City Race Course. *Photo: David Rosen.*

My father stumbles toward me
and tucks a casino chip into my palm.
While cicadas croon from the seagrass,
a mangy kitten bathes herself.

Someone should take her home.

Chapter 44

GHOSTS OF ATLANTIC CITY

Puneet Dutt

it is not macau
nor is it vegas.

    it is the AC
wind-whipped and sandy-
beached,
where the weight of history hangs
    not just on gamblers.

at eighteen, I opened my eyes to
the postcards, the films, the history
books
i had seen
come alive in front of me —
    and its ghosts —
    some still playing slots
    in hats of
    felt and velvet and bird feathers
    bright—
turn and watch me,

Bonnie Gordon and her son **Albert**
pose for a souvenir photo. *Courtesy of
Leesa Toscano.*

a handful of old coins sweating
in see-through hands,
bristling in high-necked cotton
and lace.

the living move among the dead on
the electric boardwalk,
        waiting to pull more in.

there is an energy here
and deep, deep history.
it is not macau, nor is it vegas.
it is the AC,
Atlantic City,
where the living dance with ghosts.

ABOUT THE EDITORS

*L*eesa Toscano is a writer, poet and Atlantic City native who has worked in casinos and hotels for many years and currently works for the Atlantic County government. She has been published in poetry anthologies and has published a children's title called *Eat Your Vegetables* (Publish America, 2012). Leesa spends her time away from working and writing advocating and volunteering with local arts organizations. She is an actress who has appeared in many films and plays in the Atlantic City area. Her standup comedy routine has appeared locally and in Atlantic City and New York.

*J*anet Robinson Bodoff is a retired newspaper reporter and graphic designer from Ventnor City. Her work has appeared in the *Philadelphia Inquirer*, *Philadelphia Bulletin*, *Philadelphia Journal*, *Rolling Stone*, *Concert Magazine* and more. Her poetry has appeared in several poetry anthologies. Janet has directed many arts organizations and served on the board of directors for many others. She is a writer, poet, artist, silversmith and teacher. She finds it difficult to sit still and do nothing.